Competing on Culture

About The Futures Series on Community Colleges

The Futures Series on Community Colleges is designed to produce and deliver books that strike to the heart of issues that will shape the future of community colleges. Futures books examine emerging structures, systems, and business models and stretch prevailing assumptions about leadership and management by reaching beyond the limits of convention and tradition.

Topics addressed in the series are those that are vital to community colleges, but have yet to receive meaningful attention in literature, research, and analysis. Futures books are written by scholars and practitioners who deliver a unique perspective on a topic or issue—a president or higher education consultant bringing expert and practical understanding to a topic, a policy analyst breaking down a complex problem into component parts, an academic or think tank scholar conducting incisive research, or a researcher and a practitioner working together to examine an issue through different lenses.

Futures books are developed on the premise that disruptive innovation and industry transformation are, and will be, an ongoing challenge. Gradual improvement is, understandably, a natural preference of leaders. It will not be enough, however, to position our colleges for the future. The future will be about transformation and, to perform optimally, our colleges will need to become capable of large-scale change. As leaders come face-to-face with digital forces and rapidly changing social, economic, and public policy conditions, they will have no choice but to get ahead of change or relinquish market position to competitors. Futures books are a vehicle through which leaders can learn about and prepare for what's ahead. Whether it's through analysis of what big data will mean in the next generation of colleges or which business models will become the new normal, Futures books are a resource for practitioners who realize that the ideas of out-of-the-box thinkers and the innovative practices of high performing organizations can be invaluable for answering big questions and solving complex problems.

Richard L. Alfred, Series Founding Editor, Emeritus Professor of Higher Education, University of Michigan

Debbie L. Sydow, Series Senior Editor, President, Richard Bland College of the College of William and Mary

Kate Thirolf, Series Editor, Dean of Business and Human Services, Jackson College

Books in The Futures Series on Community Colleges

Developing Tomorrow's Leaders: Context, Challenges, and Capabilities
By Pamela Eddy, Debbie L. Sydow, Richard L. Alfred, and Regina L. Garza Mitchell
This book provides a template for leadership development in the community college sector. The theme of the book focuses on the need to move beyond hierarchical leadership to networked leadership that taps talent throughout the institution. The transformational change required in the two-year sector demands new approaches to leading, including tolerance for risk, use of data analytics, and a focus on relationships. New and alternative means for leadership development are presented.

The Urgency of Now: Equity and Excellence
By Marcus M. Kolb, Samuel D. Cargile, et al.
The Urgency of Now asserts that in addition to being granted access to the community college, all 21st-century students need uncompromised support to succeed. Success means demonstrating relevant learning for transfer and employment and timely completion of credentials. Looking to the future, the authors contend that community colleges, both by their past successes and future challenges, are at the epicenter for determining the essential ingredients of a new student-centered system that guarantees equity and excellence.

Unrelenting Change, Innovation, and Risk: Forging the Next Generation of Community Colleges
By Daniel J. Phelan
In this book, thirty-five-year veteran Dan Phelan shares key insights from his personal and professional journey as a transformational, entrepreneurial community college leader. The book's wisdom and insights are amplified by observations gleaned from interviews and visits with dozens of leading practitioners. Drawing upon his sailing experiences, Phelan argues that leaders should stop playing it safe in the harbor because the real gains driving institutional and student success are found in uncharted waters. *Unrelenting Change, Innovation, and Risk* dares community college leaders to innovate and provides them with a tool kit for understanding changing conditions, assessing risk, and successfully navigating change.

Financing Community Colleges: Where We Are, Where We're Going
By Richard Romano and James Palmer
Grounded in an economic perspective, *Financing Community Colleges* helps college leaders make sense of the challenges they face in securing and managing the resources needed to carry out the community college mission. Finance has perpetually been an Achilles' heel for leaders at all levels of management. With the premise that leaders are better at winning battles they know something about, this book equips leaders with an understand-

ing of the fundamentals and the complexities of community college finance. It tackles current and emerging issues with insight that is analytic and prophetic—a must-read for current and prospective leaders.

Previously Published Books in The Future Series on Community Colleges

Minding the Dream: The Process and Practice of the American Community College, Second Edition, by Gail O. Mellow and Cynthia M. Heelan

First in the World: Community Colleges and America's Future, by J. Noah Brown

Community College Student Success: From Boardrooms to Classrooms, by Banessa Smith Morest

Re-visioning Community Colleges, by Debbie Sydow and Richard Alfred

Community Colleges on the Horizon: Challenge, Choice, or Abundance, by Richard Alfred, Christopher Shults, Ozan Jaquette, and Shelley Strickland

Competing on Culture

Driving Change in Community Colleges

Randall VanWagoner

Series Founding Editor: Richard L. Alfred
Series Senior Editor: Debbie L. Sydow
Series Editor: Kate Thirolf

ROWMAN & LITTLEFIELD
Lanham • Boulder • New York • London

Published by Rowman & Littlefield
An imprint of The Rowman & Littlefield Publishing Group, Inc.
4501 Forbes Boulevard, Suite 200, Lanham, Maryland 20706
www.rowman.com

Unit A, Whitacre Mews, 26-34 Stannary Street, London SE11 4AB

British Library Cataloguing in Publication Information Available

Library of Congress Cataloging-in-Publication Data

Names: VanWagoner, Randall, author.
Title: Competing on culture : driving change in community colleges / Randall VanWagoner.
Description: Lanham : Rowman & Littlefield, [2018] | Series: The futures series on community
    colleges | Includes bibliographical references and index.
Identifiers: LCCN 2018001993 (print) | LCCN 2018011041 (ebook) | ISBN 9781475834024 (elec-
    tronic) | ISBN 9781475834000 (cloth : alk. paper) | ISBN 9781475834017 (pbk. : alk. paper)
Subjects: LCSH: Community colleges—United States—Administration. | Mohawk Valley Commu-
    nity College.
Classification: LCC LB2328.15.U6 (ebook) | LCC LB2328.15.U6 V26 2018 (print) | DDC 378.1/
    5430973—dc23
LC record available at https://lccn.loc.gov/2018001993

Printed in the United States of America

Contents

Foreword

In 1947, the Truman Commission called for the expansion of a network of public community colleges to advance democracy and sustain the republic by providing access to higher education for Americans—to "meet the total post-high school needs of its community." These colleges embraced this call to action, and from those humble beginnings it is hard to believe now that America's community colleges now serve nearly half of all undergraduates in this country in over 1,100 institutions.

It's even harder to imagine what many of these organizations have become: highly complex and intentionally responsive drivers of economic and social mobility in the communities they serve. Distinctly American, these organizations reflect the hopes and calculus of a nation that recognized its strength and vitality would best be measured by the way it provided education as an opportunity for its residents. Community colleges boast their flexibility, agility, and nimbleness (so much so that these exact words dominate the ethos of most community college strategic plans) in driving workforce development, enhancing community capacity-building, and serving the underserved in their communities. Adaptability and stewardship are our hallmarks, stretching and growing to do what our community needs us to do with the resources it invests in us.

What may have not been anticipated are the distinctive characteristics of sense-making that have settled in these institutions of educational mobility—and the demands that would be placed on them as our country continues to grapple with its own identity and inherent struggles of power, privilege, and access; the micro and macro communities that compose this union and the inherent challenges in serving them all equitably within a college; and the inevitable competition for resources to deliver such a noble and necessary mission in an economic and fiscal environment where there are multiple actors, demands, and needs. Redesigning, reinventing, and resetting them-selves in response to these forces has not come without a cost for community colleges: *many now find themselves in a crucible moment where our ability to transform and perform yet again is constrained in large parts by the leadership, culture, and inertia of the very organizations we have become.*

Calls for enhanced completion outcomes and expanded success rates for traditionally underrepresented students coupled with robust and, at times, unclear expectations and influences defined by external stakeholders has created a unique and defining moment for community colleges. Equitable and inclusive community college environments that advance degree attain-ment, propel transfer success, and document postgraduate employment placement are not just desired; they are expected. Uncertain and unprece-dented underinvestment in public support for higher education is at an all-time high. It is no surprise, then, that navigating and leading highly complex organizations with compelling access missions and high-stakes outcome ex-pectations can be immensely challenging.

Considerable energy and expertise are needed to best prepare the commu-nity college—its culture, its leadership, and its employees—for the forward-facing reality of now. How do college leaders craft compelling and action-able student success visions for their organizations? How do leaders diag-nose, navigate, and use organizational culture to successfully advance stu-dent success reform work? How do colleges engage and move faculty and staff to leadership roles in student success reform efforts within their organ-izations? How do college leaders lift organizations to meet the demands of legislative decision-makers, grant makers, regulatory and accrediting bodies, and other invested external stakeholders? And most important to all of this, how can colleges position themselves in the midst of the swirl happening around them, to them, and for them?

This exploration by VanWagoner is both timely and necessary as the nature of academic work is being stretched and challenged for America's community colleges—and I thank him for the intellectual curiosity grounded in experience and outcomes that drives this book.

DeRionne P. Pollard, PhD
President, Montgomery College (MD)

Preface

Culture as an Organizational Lever

Community colleges are under intense pressure to transform in an environment best described by the words "change or die." Changing demographics, advancing technology, heightened demands for accountability, funding constraints, and frame-breaking competitors have combined to create an environment in which transformation is an ongoing imperative. Stakeholders have accentuated the transformation imperative through simultaneously contradictory demands for more and better service and more efficient use of resources. Knowingly or unknowingly, they have created a new mantra—more *and better* with less.

These forces have changed the work environment in community colleges. Pulled in competing directions by events beyond their control, staff splinter into functional units operating independently from one another. Culture—once an umbrella for leaders and staff working toward shared goals of access and growth—breaks down into microcultures pulled in different directions by competing demands.

Leaders who in earlier times took only a passive interest in culture now find it a formidable barrier to change as staff dig in and cling to established ways of doing things. Culture is not more resistant to change today than it was twenty or thirty years ago. Rather, community colleges are pursuing change in an increasingly complex environment with currents and countercurrents that leave little room for error.

Whether it be fundamental changes to advance the student success agenda, responding to workforce demands, or addressing community needs, community colleges are faced with the reality of transforming from quiet, accessible community assets to more prominent anchor institutions that drive economic and community development in their service areas. Healthy cultures are central to the decision making that makes transformation possible and must be better understood in this era of fundamental change.

Further complicating the capacity of colleges to achieve transformation is a cultural evolution that gives the illusion, but not the reality, of transformation. Small change is not sufficient to keep community colleges ahead of competitors. More is necessary, and the "more" is transformation—a process driven by intentional and deliberate actions of high-performing cultures that fuel and finish change with tangible results. Yet, as important as capacity for transformation is to the future viability of community colleges, it is ironic that missing in community college literature and research is a comprehensive and practical understanding of the manner in which organizational culture acts as a lever for and against change.

The old saw "culture eats strategy for breakfast" epitomizes the importance of culture as a means for enhancing the long-term viability of an organization. Little is available in the way of resources for community college leaders seeking a better understanding of organizational culture and its effect on change. The sector-specific literature is dated and offers little in the way of useful insights for leaders involved in building and shaping culture. Accordingly, a practical examination of what culture is and how it actually works in community colleges is long overdue and necessary.

Three questions critical to the relationship between culture and change guide the flow of this book:

1. What aspects of organizational culture propel or inhibit community colleges in the pursuit of change?
2. What are the attributes of organizations with healthy cultures?
3. How do community colleges use culture to promote and manage change and position the institution for the future?

MY APPROACH

I was inspired to write this book because organizational culture fascinates me. Having worked in four different community colleges in four different states, I found community colleges to be all so very different and so very much the same. Culture seems to be everywhere in the organization and simultaneously nowhere, with people carrying various perceptions of what culture is and what it means.

We spend the majority of our waking hours working together at our jobs in our colleges for our students and communities. This reality is a call to action for us to spend more time and attention toward understanding existing culture and identifying ways to intentionally and productively shape a preferred future culture in our colleges.

The literature on organizational culture is mostly conceptual and distant from the daily realities leaders experience on campus. Perhaps because culture is unique to each organization, the challenge is to coherently explore the common attributes and most useful levers for transforming culture. A practical examination of what is needed to drive organizational change through culture is the guiding force and inspiration for this book.

To inform my writing of this book, I drew on my direct research over the past two years as well as my learning and experiences over the past twenty-six years of working in community colleges. While I share examples from my experience, they are intended to simply illustrate the concepts I put forth throughout the book. Regarding specific examples at Mohawk Valley Community College, they represent a work in progress that is far from perfect, but hopefully illustrate a number of key elements in place that we work on while collectively trying to get a little better every day.

I fully recognize that many elements I explore in the book are present at community colleges across the country. However, the challenge for all of us is to develop, refine, and execute many of these variables—using them as fundamental levers for transformation in our respective cultures to make our colleges as outstanding as our students and communities need them to be!

Acknowledgments

Heartfelt thanks go to my coeditors Drs. Richard Alfred and Debbie Sydow for their time, support, and guidance with this book. I simply could not have done it without their talent, expertise, and encouragement. And special thanks to Dr. Alfred. Dick has been a career-long mentor, advisor, and friend. No one has shaped my professional trajectory more than he has, and I am forever indebted to him for his unwavering belief in my abilities and countless opportunities for me to stretch and grow.

I so appreciate Dr. Linda Bowman for her willingness, skill, and courage to take the time to provide me with critical feedback on the earliest of drafts of this manuscript. Her critique, insights, and encouragement were incredibly valuable. Thank you.

I'm eternally grateful for the support of my family. Endless thanks to my wife, Jennifer, who makes me who I want to be. She is my partner, love, best friend, and conscience, whose support throughout my career and this process has been valuable beyond measure. Thanks to our daughters, Lauren and Emily, who provide me with joy, love, and inspiration to give my best toward everything I do. And thanks to my parents for providing me with a great upbringing, believing in me before I believed in myself, and for their eternal love, interest, and support in all my endeavors.

Sincere thanks go to the Mohawk Valley Community College Board of Trustees for their support and guidance that has challenged and motivated me in so many productive ways over the years. Thanks also to my incredible Cabinet team and officemates who make it so easy to come to work each day. And thanks to the faculty, administration, staff, and students of MVCC who make me proud and humbled to serve such a fine institution and community.

I thank the numerous mentors and friends that have given me so much over the years. In particular, Jackie Andrews, for piquing my interest in organizational culture (and the importance of living a meaningful life) so early in my career; Dorothy Horrell, for providing me with an inspiring model of what a great leader looks like and how they make others feel; Randy Schmailzl, for giving me so many opportunities to grow and learn from his unique and exceptional leadership style; Pat Carter, for her ever-present calming influence and timely guidance throughout my career; and Idahlynn Karre, for her teachings, encouragement, and friendship.

—Randall J. VanWagoner

Note: All revenue that I receive from the sale of this book will go to the Mohawk Valley Community College Foundation to support innovation and student success.

Introduction

This book is organized in a way that builds a logical narrative for understanding culture and how to identify key levers to transform organizational culture in community colleges. The organizing flow of the chapters is based in my belief that leadership can create trust and connections that build a sense of community to productively develop a culture of inquiry and inform the culture in ways to anticipate the future and thrive in disruptive times.

Chapter 1 provides a detailed review of the characteristics and components that comprise organizational culture. Strategies for assessing and understanding culture are reviewed to set the stage for taking action to change culture. A comparison of functional and dysfunctional cultures allows for the discussion of what levers can be used in what ways to prompt both positive and negative change in cultures.

Three illuminating case studies comprise chapter 2, with stories of how three very different community colleges were able to transform their respective cultures over extended periods of time. With presidents in the three cases serving fifteen-, twenty-five-, and twenty-nine-year tenures, the arc of transformation is markedly different and yet inherently similar. An extensive Lessons Learned section at the end of the chapter weaves together common and enduring truths about cultural transformation.

Chapter 3 highlights leadership models and identifies key behaviors that align with the requirements to effect cultural change described in the remaining chapters of the book. Aspects of paradox, philosophical alignment of leaders at all levels of the organization, and the importance of managing the scale and pace of change are all examined in depth. The chapter closes with an exploration into the importance of leading for equity and inclusion to truly transform organizational culture for the future.

Going beyond employee engagement to develop employee investment and build cultures into communities is the focus of chapter 4. Key aspects of organizational life are highlighted in this chapter, including the importance of trust and transparency, new employee hiring and onboarding, roles and responsibilities, governance, professional development, evaluations, rewards, and recognition.

Chapter 5 focuses on creating a culture of inquiry. Building on the key leadership behaviors outlined in chapter 3 and many concepts introduced in chapter 4, this chapter takes culture transformation further through the infusion of data and inquiry. Aspects of setting the stage and making the case for why and how data are used are explored in depth. Through my experiences at midsize and large community colleges and having started my career in institutional research, I offer considerations for how to build and strengthen infrastructure to support a culture of inquiry.

Chapter 6 closes the book out with considerations into the future of community colleges and what community colleges might do to position themselves for success. The chapter explores the need to rethink structure and power in the midst of ever-increasing disruptive forces creating significant pressure points for our colleges. The closing lens for the chapter and the book highlights the need, for survival in the future, for community colleges to become far more entrepreneurial and move from simply responding to change to intentionally anticipating change.

Chapter One

Understanding Culture

If you get the culture right, most of the other stuff will just take care of itself.
—Tony Hsieh, CEO of Zappos.com

Organizational culture is like a river. It is in constant motion and yet maintains a distinct and ever-forward flow. Every river has a story with a beginning that precedes countless changes—whether subtle or sudden—that comprise its current features. As with culture, every newcomer enters the river from a different place, never able to enter the same point twice in the ongoing current. Likewise, those who stand in the river for a long time struggle to describe it—they just know they are in it.

And so it goes with culture. Like a river, culture shapes the organizational landscape around it, determining where the curves, narrows, and falls are. It has deep pockets that are not easy to see or understand, as well as shallow areas that can attract debris and unwanted material. Sudden violent storms and flash floods of significant disruption can dramatically alter its route while drought and a dearth of resources can test its resilience and ultimate survival. And like the fast-moving whitewater rapids found in some rivers, the rough periods that occur within a culture can cause great uncertainty.

These certainly are uncertain times for America's community colleges, and culture has become increasingly vital to maintaining the ever-forward momentum community colleges have enjoyed to this point in time. More than any other attribute, culture reflects the past and present of an organization and as well as its future. It is a convenient way of explaining the unexplainable—when things go bad or inaction prevails, "It's the culture."

Logical solutions to problems can be proposed and bold initiatives mounted only to run into the impenetrable wall of culture. In the space between ideas and action, culture can easily become an excuse for inaction.

Facing swirling forces of change and burdened with entrenched cultures, leaders default to what is doable rather than what is critical. Organizational culture does not change overnight—a reality that leaders committed to change discover soon after taking office. It takes years, in some instances a decade or more, to meaningfully change culture. Most leaders do not have that kind of time and end up rushing a process that moves at its own pace. Hence, one could postulate that, similar to strategy, "Culture eats leaders for breakfast."

With historical artifacts rooted in four-year colleges and universities (administrative structures) and secondary schools (instructors and teaching emphasis), community colleges are subject to ambiguity when it comes to influences on organizational culture.[1] Currents and crosscurrents of societal change are creating a dynamic environment for organizational behavior, yet the cultural norms of most community colleges are rooted in the traditional hierarchy and are as difficult to change as ever.

Without intentional effort, culture in community colleges is likely to continue the legacy of slow, protracted decision-making mired in silos of politicized departments and the worst aspects of shared governance. More troubling is the way in which community colleges have generally spent the last thirty years gently working around the edges of culture with regard to assessment and the use of data, while often avoiding fundamental change. Community colleges are plagued by these attributes of carry-over culture that are no longer viable.

Saying that community colleges are responsive because they can develop a new workforce development program in less than twelve months is too narrow and shortsighted. Responsiveness worked in previous environments characterized by stability and linear change. As change has become nonlinear and the environment more unstable, everything about the operation requires questioning and rethinking that makes cultural transformation essential.

With significant shifts in the external environment intensifying pressure from all angles, community colleges are ripe for cultural transformation. Decision-making needs to accelerate, which will require new structures that complement a modern iteration of shared governance and more sophisticated and transparent approaches for using data analytics to drive meaningful change. Community colleges need to embrace the disruption and speed at which change is occurring by moving from a responsive organization to an anticipatory culture.

Cultural change is challenging and complex. As Cameron and Quinn state,

> When the values, orientations, definitions, and goals stay constant—even when procedures and strategies are altered—organizations return quickly to the status quo. The same is true for individuals. Personality types, personal

styles, and behavioral habits rarely change significantly, despite programs to induce change such as diets, exercise regimens, or motivational seminars. Without an alteration of the fundamental goals, values, and expectations of organizations or individuals, change remains superficial and of short duration.[2]

Culture remains the dominant variable in organizational change. Organizational realities are hampered by deeply embedded patterns of more stable times that are no longer viable in the disruptive nonlinear state of current and future environments. The essential question therefore becomes, "Who or what is shaping your organizational culture and what levers are being used to change it?"

CULTURE DEFINED

"Simply stated, organizational culture is the way people think and act. Every organization has a culture, which either works for or against change—and it can make the difference between success and failure."[3] Culture is the vehicle through which organizational members define reality through shared beliefs and interpretations of daily and regular happenings.[4] As Schein states in his seminal work on organizational culture, it is "a pattern of basic assumptions—invented, discovered, or developed by a given group as it learns to cope with problems of external adaptation and internal integration—that have worked well enough to be considered valid and, therefore, to be taught to new members as the correct way to perceive, think, and feel in relation to those problems."[5] The key is to raise awareness of those patterns and leverage culture for necessary organizational change.

Understanding Culture

To gain insight into organizational culture, leaders entering an organization typically follow a pattern of scheduling listening sessions to assess the organization, pull together a representative group to define and confirm organizational issues, and update the strategic plan. Too often, however, leaders develop strategy and pursue change without understanding the underlying dynamics of organizational culture.

Uncovering and understanding basic elements of culture within a college is critical to developing a successful strategy. This dynamic can be mitigated by recognizing what Kempner calls, "webs of significance" that are defined by "norms, values, beliefs, symbols, and myths members bring to the organization that over time form its character."[6] Different webs are at work in programmatic areas of community colleges—occupational and career education, general education and transfer, basic skills and continuing education.

Webs also form among employees representing different groups in community colleges—full-time in contrast to part-time instructors, credit in contrast to noncredit instructors—and contrasts among administrative groups in different departments.[7] Webs committed to different intentions, sometimes contradictory, can wreak havoc on culture depending on the extent of divergence in normative outlook among and between groups. It doesn't take much to figure out why culture is such an influential force in change. It is the single most important mechanism impacting the ability of an institution to transform.[8]

Leaders come and go, initiatives are launched and abandoned, and services are added and adjusted, but culture remains. I was part of a profound experience in a faculty focus group many years ago in an institution engaged in a strategic plan update. To get things underway, the president asked participants to draw a picture of how they envisioned the college in twenty years. When we went around the room to share our drawings, an art faculty member quickly stood up and described her drawing:

> Here is the main entrance to the college. All the little people walking through the front doors—those are all the administrators who have come and gone over the years and will continue to come and go in the future. See the people in the window? Those are the faculty and staff—we've always been here and we'll still be here in the future no matter what.

That is culture.

The study of culture can involve perspective rooted in anthropology by viewing culture as something an organization "is" or through a sociological lens by viewing it as something an organization "has."[9] Either way, culture is layered with tangible and intangible elements that shape behavior of individuals within an organization and influence outcomes in significant ways.

Cultures can be greatly influenced by formal and informal forms of power that develop uniquely based on faculty dynamics in departments. Not infrequently, union and governance leadership roles are filled by a succession of faculty from the same department—in one college it may be business; in another social sciences; and in yet another, life sciences faculty provide the loudest and most influential faculty voice. The predisposition of faculty and their outlook on organizational behavior have significant influence on cultural norms and whether change is blocked, stalled, or advanced. "Individual actions and behavior, when thought of as a nest of cultural behavior, have a pervasive influence on institutional life."[10]

Leaders entering an organization and seeking an understanding of culture are confronted all too quickly with a phenomenon that defies simple comprehension. Understanding culture is a complex undertaking. It calls for leaders to "listen to the organization" and think of it as a living organism with innate behaviors and systems that operate automatically and require diagnosis, patience, and care. Analysis of organizational behavior like socialization of new members, how information is owned and shared, formal and informal leadership structures, and decision-making processes related to operations and strategy can provide important insights into organizational culture.[11]

Assessing Culture

Instruments have been developed for mapping culture. One such instrument is the Organizational Culture Assessment Instrument (OCAI), which provides an analytical overview of the makeup of an organization's culture.[12] Based on the competing values framework,[13] the OCAI identifies four types of cultures based on a unique configuration of six elements: dominant characteristics, organizational leadership, management of employees, organizational glue, strategic emphases, and criteria for success.

The four types of culture are identified as clan (characterized by informal collaboration), hierarchy (characterized by formal rules and control), adhocracy (characterized by high levels of flexibility and external focus), and market (characterized by a drive to successfully compete). While the OCAI can help diagnose a culture, nine steps are suggested to develop change strategies that fit a specific culture:

1. Reach consensus regarding the current organizational culture.
2. Reach consensus regarding the preferred future organizational culture.
3. Determine what change will and will not mean.
4. Identify stories illustrating the desired future culture.
5. Identify a strategic action agenda.
6. Identify immediate small wins.
7. Identify leadership implications.
8. Identify metrics, measures, and milestones to maintain accountability.
9. Identify a communication strategy.[14]

Whether a leader pursues full implementation of the OCAI or simply uses these nine action steps as a guide, gauging the makeup of culture through an analytical tool is an important step in cultural change. Engaging faculty and staff in a dialogue about culture as it exists and as it should be raises overall awareness of the importance of culture among organizational stakeholders. Leveraging the power of stories to illustrate and amplify elements of culture can shape an action agenda that creates small wins and success measures that can be communicated and used throughout the organization to guide ongoing development of cultures that embrace change.

Having said this, it is not productive to view culture as something that has to be fixed. Culture is best viewed as the by-product of structures, processes, and systems that are enacted and modified over time in an organization. As Lorsch and McTague state, "Culture is not the culprit. It makes sense to look at culture as an outcome—not a cause or a fix. Organizations are complex systems with ripple effects. Reworking fundamental practices will inevitably lead to new values and behaviors."[15] Changing the rhythm of the organization by altering fundamental practices is a beginning point for the process of cultural change.

Components of Culture

Understanding and working with the organizational culture requires an exploration of the primary components in an organization that shape it (see table 1.1). The organizational profile of a college is comprised of "givens" that comprise the foundation for culture—when and how a college was founded, where it is located, the community it serves, and the profile of stakeholders. Other characteristics that shape culture include leadership, governance, programs and services, and elements that can be manipulated to change culture. Finally, organizational adaptability—the capacity to anticipate change and adapt accordingly—is an important component shaping the culture of any college.

Organizational Profile

As simplistic as it may seem, the profile of an organization has a substantial impact on culture. Community colleges cannot delete elements of their history, they cannot change their location, and they cannot alter fundamental characteristics of the community they serve.

History

The history of a college and the organizational story developing over time is a powerful contributor to organizational culture. Leaders will do well to

Table 1.1.   Components of Culture

Organizational Profile (Static)	Key Characteristics (Malleable)
History	Leadership
Location	Structure and governance
Community	Processes and systems
Employee Profile	Programs and services
Student Profile	Data usage and analytics
Institutional Size	Adaptability, external focus, and future orientation

understand the "founding story" that endures in the history of the organization.[16] Organizational culture is very different in a community college established as a technical institute compared to one founded as a junior college. A technical-oriented college typically has closer ties to employers and workforce needs while a transfer-oriented college is more likely to focus on tending to issues that reinforce a commitment to the traditions of higher education and transfer opportunities.

Similarly, the age of a college—the "length" of its history—is a contributor to culture as well. The relative youth of American community colleges is significant, as cultures in colleges formed one hundred years ago or earlier differ in significant ways from cultures in those formed five decades ago—and differ even more from those in which founding faculty are still on staff.

Key events in a college's history and evolution shape culture in meaningful ways. For example, if a college moved from quarters to semesters at some point, opened a branch campus, implemented a massive reorganization, or endured a painful and protracted period of leadership instability, the impact on the culture may linger for years in the form of a pivotal story. As Sturt and Nordstrom state, "Pivotal stories expose the thinking that overcame the situation. They focus on the first big win, or the first big challenge, that was overcome. Pivotal stories share the history and the mindset of how an organization deals with change."[17]

Community

Community colleges mirror the communities they serve. Colleges reflect the community profile, which can be liberal or conservative; blue collar or white collar; homogenous or diverse; wealthy, poor, or somewhere in between; upbeat and positive or downtrodden and pessimistic; or possess a collective mind-set of growth or scarcity.[18] Community characteristics influence everything from student and employee demographics to the programs and services a college provides to meet community needs.

The community context is particularly critical in colleges with local control where a substantial portion of a college's operating or capital revenue is generated by local bond levies that must be approved by a public vote or an allocation requiring the approval of a county legislature. If taxpayers or elected officials are not supportive or adopt a particular fixed mind-set about a college, resources can grow scarce and severely limit the vitality of a community college.

Employee and Student Profile

Influenced by the location and community expectations of a college, employee and student demographics are primary shapers of organizational culture. Students shape programs and services. Low-income students, for example, have different program and service needs compared to students with more economic means. Employee demographics shape culture through years of service. Many colleges have "bulges" of faculty and staff on a continuum of service resulting from retirement of founding cohorts or faculty and staff hiring during periods of enrollment growth. Larger cohorts serve as rings on the tree of organizational culture that may assert influence on the culture due to shared experiences and interpretations of institutional behavior.

Institutional Size

Institutional size shapes organizational culture through the level of complexity and extent of connectivity among faculty and staff throughout the organization. This dynamic plays out in the role of subcultures that are more numerous and diverse in larger colleges, many of which are multicampus. Larger institutions differ in complexity from smaller institutions where faculty and staff are more closely connected to the center of the institution.

For example, in a multicampus institution, many employees may rarely, if ever, visit campuses other than the one on which they work, and the organization feels like a series of loosely connected islands. In contrast, smaller institutions have more deeply connected cultures with artifacts that reflect more intimate ties, like e-mails sent to all employees whenever someone has a baby or a death in the family.

KEY CHARACTERISTICS

While the organizational profile contains elements that are not easily changed, other factors contributing to culture can be altered and shaped to transform culture.

Leadership

Although leadership will be discussed more specifically in another chapter, it is a key factor in shaping organizational culture. Leadership can influence culture through formal and informal means. Senior administrators, for better or worse, can have an enormous impact on the culture of an organization through strategic decisions, daily actions, and ongoing behavior. Senior leaders set the tone for the organization and are under constant scrutiny.

They can carry the day when times are tough and inspire resilience throughout the organization with clear and reassuring messages and actions. In stark contrast, senior leaders can also demoralize a culture through repeated reminders of scarce resources or the need to improve with no vision of where to go or how to get there.

Informal leaders throughout the organization shape culture by interpreting organizational behavior in ways that influence others and, more subtly, through informal interaction with peers and subordinates. They may not be the ones chairing committee meetings, but they always find a way for their voices to be heard. Informal leaders typically have a knack for sifting through the noise and finding workable space between the din of the naysayers and the sometimes detached rhetoric of senior administrators.

Informal leaders never eat lunch alone and have naturally cultivated wide networks at all levels of the organization. With their value often undervalued and unrecognized, informal leaders could be far more influential for positive change if formal leaders engaged them in more intentional ways. Informal leaders are what Meyerson calls "tempered radicals."

> Tempered radicals bear no banners; they sound no trumpets. Their ends are sweeping, but their means are mundane. They are firm in their commitments, yet flexible in the ways they fulfill them. Their actions may be small but can spread like a virus. They yearn for rapid change but trust in patience. They often work individually yet pull people together. Instead of stridently pressing their agendas, they start conversations. Rather than battling powerful foes, they seek powerful friends. And in the face of setbacks, they keep going. To do all this, tempered radicals understand revolutionary change for what it is—a phenomenon that can occur suddenly but more often than not requires time, commitment, and the patience to endure.[19]

Structure and Governance

The extent to which an organizational chart is centralized or decentralized defines the number of administrative layers through which decisions are made and supervisory and departmental relationships are defined. A more loosely coupled structure operates in an ad hoc fashion permitting individuals and groups latitude in communication and decision-making. Contrast this with communication and decision-making patterns in tightly coupled bureaucratic organizations that confine interaction to bounded channels.[20] Whether loose or tight, structure shapes culture.

The scope of responsibility and authority plays a role in culture by the sheer number of direct reports supervisors have. An academic dean supervising fifty full-time faculty operates in a very different subculture than one supervising twenty faculty. Tradeoffs exist with different structures. For example, a narrow organizational chart of five deans supervising two hundred full-time faculty might facilitate the development of more efficient systems of staffing, scheduling, and other processes. However, such broad organization can greatly diminish the strength of departmental subcultures and attention to detail.

In contrast, a more generous ratio of supervisory responsibility—say ten deans or department heads for those same two hundred full-time faculty—is likely to facilitate stronger departmental subcultures and closer connections. The tradeoff in this structure is the risk of departments creating their own processes and variations that eventually lead to a breakdown of systems, inefficient operations, and diluting of resources. These tradeoffs underscore the need to consider periodic strategic structural modifications so the downsides of whatever current structure is in place does not breed deep dysfunction that becomes harder to undo over time.

A college's governance system parallels and complements administrative structure through the manner in which decisions are made. An inclusive governance model involving many parts of the organization in decision processes has an entirely different feel compared to a culture in which information is shared on a limited basis and small issues become contentious because those without formal decision-making authority feel powerless and take issue with decisions they feel they cannot support, mainly because of processes and misunderstanding.

Governance can be a major signal for the tenor and tone of culture at a college. If disconnects exist between senior administration and the primary governance body (often some kind of senate or council), the overall culture is likely to be muted, tense, and divisive. Communications are strained and information is not widely distributed, so assumptions are based on hearsay and incorrect insights.

However, if senior administrators are actively engaged with the primary governance body and nurture the overall governance system, the culture will likely be more healthy and vibrant. Engagement can take the form of leaders carefully managing inclusive decision-making processes, intentionally closing the loop on committee recommendations, and regularly injecting useful and timely information into the governance system to increase communication, trust, and connection that nurture positive attributes for a healthy, functional, and high-performing culture.

Processes and Systems

Similar to organizational structure and governance, an institution's processes and systems are both an offshoot of and a contributor to culture. Cumbersome processes are indicative of a culture bound by inertia and challenged by change. Process "owners" committed to tried-and-true ways of performing activities scuttle change by digging in and resisting efforts to do things differently. *Every* college has process "owners" and everyone in the organization knows who they are. Leaders in the Offices of the Registrar, Financial Aid, Human Resources, Business/Bursar, Information Technology, and others can create fundamental pivot points that inherently define the perceived, and sometimes actual, levels of flexibility that characterize a culture. Contrast process-moribund organizations with process-streamlined organizations in which systems are designed with the end user in mind. Cultures in these organizations are distinguished by characteristics of adaptability and stakeholder focus that encourage openness to, and acceptance of, change.

Programs and Services

Programs and services are an obvious contributor to organizational culture. The culture of a community college with residence halls and athletics has a different feel than that of a college without these features. Colleges with extensive extracurricular offerings will likely have a more vibrant student life on campus and a more traditional culture complete with more school spirit and student engagement than a strictly commuter-oriented culture.

Another variable influencing culture is outreach. The culture of a college with extensive outreach services to underserved, disenfranchised populations in an inner city will possess different features of culture than one that serves suburban populations with a higher socioeconomic status. A college with a more diverse and low-income student population is more likely than one located in an affluent suburb to have services that address basic needs like housing and food insecurities, as well as English as a Second Language programs that facilitate increased diversity on campus—which ultimately also influences the overall culture of the organization.

Program mix can influence the culture as well. The culture of a college with comprehensive workforce and technical programs will have different elements of culture than a college more narrowly focused on transfer programs. When a college has a substantial array of technical programs tied to local workforce needs, the culture is likely to be more outwardly focused, anticipating and responding to changes in the external environment, than one that is more transfer oriented without regular mandates to alter its program mix.

Data Usage and Analytics

Organizations that provide pervasive access to data and embrace information as a means for improvement stand in stark contrast to organizations in which data is neither valued nor used—organizations in which fear over the use of data is rampant. Cultures that routinely use and analyze data at individual, departmental, and institutional levels are more likely to respond and adapt to trends in the environment. In contrast, cultures that create barriers to data usage, let alone the use of analytics, are more likely to resist change through regular rationalizing of current reality and justifying the status quo.

For example, if data are not widely used, program review processes are likely to be weak and useless, resulting in dated, underperforming, high-cost technical programs draining resources from more valuable allocations. In contrast, when colleges have invested in their data infrastructure, information is more widely available, decisions are more informed and occur faster, and resources are allocated more efficiently, resulting in a more vibrant culture benefiting from continued reallocations and investments rather than deep cuts or spending freezes.

Adaptability, External Focus, and Future Orientation

Finally, culture can be greatly influenced by the adaptability, external focus, and future orientation of an organization. An externally focused culture is likely to be more adaptable than one focused more internally and is also more likely to anticipate changes that require organizational response. This final element is the culmination of all other malleable components that comprise culture. If senior leadership is buried in the operations and fails to nurture effective governance or invest in data infrastructure, then processes and systems become closed and cumbersome. Programs and services begin to wither on the vine and a fixed mind-set of scarcity begins to pervade the entire culture. As those realities begin to take hold, the overall focus of the organization turns increasingly inward and risk averse.

A great irony in community colleges is the large extent to which faculty and staff experience change in their daily personal lives, but come to work each day expecting things to remain the same as they have been for decades. This can be countered when senior leaders invest in professional development so an organization is more likely to have a regular infusion of new ideas, information, and perspectives that connect the college to changes in the external environment. As a result, a greater awareness of changes in the marketplace becomes more present throughout the organization. Colleges that leverage the malleable characteristics of their culture are far more likely to develop and maintain an external focus, anticipate necessary changes, and become more competitive for the benefit of their students and communities.

While an organization's profile is not subject to change, the key characteristics described here can be used as levers for cultural change. With awareness and intention, leaders can alter these characteristics to create a culture that aligns with the future needs of the organization.

CULTURE AND PARADOX

Community colleges embrace and pursue simultaneously contradictory goals, hence their designation as "paradoxical" organizations. Whether the goal is open-door or selective admissions, technical or liberal arts focus, access or completion, mission comprehensiveness or mission specificity, community colleges have paradox embedded in their DNA. If one does not understand the principle of paradox and its importance as an attribute of effectiveness, then answer the following question: How many organizational types do you know who have a capacity to simultaneously pursue traditional and nontraditional delivery, planned and spontaneous change, and quantitative and qualitative conceptions of success?[21]

Community colleges are facing new forces coming out of the Great Recession that have brought to the fore the importance of paradox. They have had to find ways to achieve growth in the face of reduction, pursue opportunity in the face of adversity, balance countervailing mind-sets of abundance and scarcity, create a sense of continuity while embracing change, balance the open-door mission with the student completion agenda, and innovate in cultures trapped in inertia.[22]

To navigate these dimensions of paradox, community colleges have borrowed from best practices in high-performing organizations with functional cultures. Fundamental among these practices are attributes of leadership, employee status and behavior, core values, commitment to change, and strategy. Functional cultures embrace paradox in all of these areas, while dysfunctional cultures get stuck through a myopic and narrow view of each attribute.

FUNCTIONAL CULTURES

It is not surprising that organizations with functional cultures thrive by effectively managing contradictory forces and, in so doing, find success where others experience failure.

Leadership—Humble *and* Driven

Functional cultures have inspired and inspiring leadership that is at once humble and driven. These organizations are not solely dependent on leaders; in fact, the strongest cultures endure and continue to thrive through leader-

Table 1.2. Functional and Dysfunctional Culture

Attribute	Functional	Dysfunctional
Leadership	Humble *and* driven	Narcissistic
Employee status	Employees *and* students	Students are primary
Core values	Clear *and* personal	Vague
Employee behavior	Assertive *and* positive	Passive-Aggressive
Strategy	Short- *and* long-term view	Reactionary
Commitment to change	Pervasive *and* varied	Isolated

ship changes, in part because of the pervasive influence of servant leadership. In *The Way We'll Be*, John Zogby concluded that people no longer want to be recognized for what they own but for who they are.[23] This shift has important implications for the workplace, as employees strive to find meaning in their work and leaders must find ways to break down traditional barriers and nurture stronger connections with employees to shape culture in ways big and small.

Leaders in functional cultures unleash energy and potential in employees by bringing passion and purpose to work. Counterintuitive to the idea of the great leader that so much has been written about, leaders in high-performing organizations model humility and modesty. They exhibit qualities of authenticity and vulnerability that open all parts of the organization to a free flow of ideas and information. As Richard Sheridan, CEO of the high-performing software company Menlo Innovations, writes in *Joy, Inc.*:

> Part of the vulnerability of not having all the answers is the humility to share your ideas with your team before they are fully formulated. These ideas are like babies. We believe they are beautiful, but often the beauty is seen in our perfectly imagined hopes for the future rather than in the reality of the moment.[24]

Humility, modesty, and vulnerability are closely related characteristics that create an environment of openness, candor, transparency, and a belief that everyone has value. As Brené Brown says, "Excellence comes from vulnerability."[25] When employees feel valued, they are empowered to think more creatively, take more responsibility, and subsequently improve their performance.

In addition to being modest, humble, and vulnerable, functional cultures have leaders, as profiled in Jim Collins's book, *Good to Great*, who are strong-willed with unwavering resolve. Collins describes them as "Level 5" leaders who do what needs to be done for the good of the organization without letting their egos get in the way. Their ambition lies squarely with the success of the organization and not with their personal success. And perhaps most importantly, their humility allows them to look outward toward people other than themselves when things go well and look inward when things go badly—what Collins calls "the window and the mirror."[26]

In *Conscious Capitalism*, Mackey and Sisodia describe the importance of conscious leaders in companies where passion and purpose drive the bottom line. "Conscious leaders seek to make a positive impact on the world through their organization. They deeply embed a sense of shared purpose, enabling people to derive meaning from work. They help people grow and evolve as individuals and as leaders in their own right, and they make tough moral choices with clarity and consistency."[27]

Employee Status—Employees *and* Students

Ask almost any organizational leader what makes the place special or what its greatest resource is and they will most likely respond, "Our people." And yet, why is it that so many workplaces are anything but special and the majority of employees do not feel anything close to being the organization's greatest resource? The answer lies in part with the disconnect between leader rhetoric and workplace reality.

Functional cultures connect words and actions by clearly communicating that employees are valued and critical to the overall success of the organization. As Mackey and Sisodia state, "Most conscious businesses consider either their customers or their team members as their most important stakeholder, but whichever they consider their highest priority, the other is almost always a close second."[28] Zingerman's Deli in Ann Arbor, Michigan—world famous for its employee-focused culture—unabashedly informs visitors that its primary customer is the employee. Happy employees deliver outstanding customer service, which means happy and satisfied customers.

Demonstrating to employees that they are valued starts with transparent and engaged leaders who build trust through consistent behavior over time. Finding ways to share success and provide context in failure keeps employees connected to the center of the institution. Finally, providing ways to promote fun in the workplace and offering comprehensive benefits beyond base financial compensation sends a message of work/life balance that puts employees at the center of the organization.

> If you want employees to take a vested interest in the bigger picture, treat them like stakeholders. When you create an environment in which "jobs" are regarded more like "investments," employees will show up with passion, productivity, and focus, making your organization more profitable.[29]

Employees as primary stakeholders might appear to be in conflict with the prevailing mantras of "the customer is always right" or "students first." Following Zingerman's Deli's lead, putting employees first—or for the unaccepting, at least on par with students—will result in students being served better than they would be by employees who do not feel valued, are not engaged, and have no investment in the mission work of the organization.

Feeling valued increases the level of positivity with which people approach their jobs. Cameron's research in the University of Michigan's Center for Positive Organizations highlights the power of positivity on performance. In research on the banking and healthcare industries, Cameron found that positivity was directly connected to organizational performance. Six characteristics appeared to be at work in high-performing organizations.

1. *Caring*: People care for, are interested in, and maintain responsibility for one another as friends.
2. *Compassionate support*: People provide support for one another, including kindness and compassion when others are struggling.
3. *Forgiveness*: People avoid blame and forgive mistakes.
4. *Inspiration*: People inspire one another at work.
5. *Meaning*: The meaningfulness of work is emphasized, and people are elevated and renewed by work.
6. *Respect, integrity, and gratitude*: People treat one another with respect and express appreciation for one another. They trust one another and maintain integrity.[30]

Additionally, researchers at Gallup have found, "Beyond communicating appreciation and providing motivation to the recognized employee, the act of recognition also sends messages to other employees about what success looks like. In this way, recognition is both a tool for personal reward and an opportunity to reinforce the desired culture of the organization to other employees."[31] These findings underscore how reinforcement of human needs for connection and feeling valued elevates individual performance, leading to collective success.

Core Values—Clear *and* Personal

In periods of change, core values are highly symbolic but critical elements of functional cultures. Core values tether a culture and enable employees to find meaning in their efforts. The extent to which an organization can clearly articulate values and reinforce them in its culture is perhaps the single most important contributor to a healthy, functional culture. In *Firms of Endearment*, the authors identified companies that outperformed companies in Collins's study that led to *Good to Great*. They did so, in part, by asking thousands of consumers about companies they "love" and analyzing their approach to satisfying stakeholders. They found that in bringing the organizational core values to life, shareholders benefited as well.[32]

A healthy organizational culture is more likely to have clearly stated values that are reinforced in multiple ways throughout the organization. In some companies like Southwest Airlines and Apple, core values fundamentally communicate *why* the organization exists and are graphically pictured throughout the organization. Sinek posits in *Start with Why* that organizations should clearly understand and communicate *why* they exist, versus simply what they do, as this "is the only way to maintain lasting success and blend innovation flexibility."[33] Clarity on the core values of an organization drives employee behavior and creates consistent patterns of interactions and decision-making throughout the organization.

Firms like Wegman's Food Markets, Patagonia, Commerce Bank, Jet-Blue, Honda, IKEA, REI, and New Balance are driven by a higher purpose beyond profit. They infuse passion in corporate strategy and transfer that passion to their stakeholders, who in turn connect to the company in a virtuous cycle of reinforcing positivity. These firms all have core values embedded in attributes of functional cultures.

For example, values such as trust, learning, integrity, transparency, respect, belonging, caring, and fun promote engagement and elevate results in healthy cultures.[34] Human nature and traditional business practice may imply that values of transparency, caring, and fun are inefficient distractions from carrying out the real business of the organization. The success of high-performing businesses over time, however, clearly demonstrates that the holistic cultures embedded in these organizations outperform the profit-motivated cultures in traditional business organizations. Paradox comes into play when organizations pursue initiatives that are contradictory to their core values. Organizations with functional cultures find ways to leverage their core values and innovate in periods of uncertainty and change to achieve high performance.

The core values at Disney are a great example of enacting a vision through a clear set of core values. Four simple values—safety, courtesy, show, and capacity—allow Disney employees to live out the organizational vision of *We create happiness.* "They are prioritized as such, and they are powerful tools in that they are easy to remember and can be used as a litmus test for excellence, whether thinking strategically, or whether acting in the moment on the front line."[35] The clarity and significance of these values help shape employee behavior to create the tremendous customer experience Disney provides to millions on an annual basis.

Employee Behavior—Assertive *and* Positive

Functional cultures have employees who communicate in emotionally intelligent, clear, and assertive ways. Communication that is characterized as assertive stops short of being aggressive and strikes a balance between saying what needs to be said and delivering the message in ways that are constructive and growth focused.

Assertive behavior also facilitates crucial conversations that lead to the management of productive conflict. Functional cultures have leaders who create a safe environment for people to create and fill a pool of shared meaning. As more information is added to the pool and the depth of shared meaning increases, the collective intelligence of the players grows and leads to greater understanding and better decisions.

This approach requires people to clarify the intent of all the actors, identify shared purpose, stating their views while remaining open to oppositional counterpoints, talking tentatively, and feeling safe to test understanding of differing views. When employees model behaviors to successfully have these crucial conversations throughout the organization, misunderstandings are minimized and issues are analyzed and resolved in productive ways that reinforce the functional aspects of the culture.[36]

Strategy—Short- *and* Long-Term

Functional cultures have a laser focus on change in the short term, while simultaneously maintaining a long-term view. Thinking of an organization as a living organism allows one to consider culture as equivalent to DNA. "An organism's DNA needs to be genetically resistant but also adaptive. Likewise, a corporate culture needs to be resistant to short-term incidental influences, but have the ability to adapt when needed."[37]

A long-term view is critical to provide stability against unforeseen challenges and opportunities. Comparing the disciplined preparation of Roald Amundsen with the risky planning of Robert Scott in their 1911 race to the South Pole, Collins applies Amundsen's twenty-mile-march approach to organizations. Amundsen traveled twenty miles per day—in good days and bad. In contrast, Scott traveled as many as forty miles on good days while not traveling at all on bad days.

Amundsen made it to the South Pole three months ahead of Scott, who perished on the return journey.[38] High-performing organizations use the twenty-mile march as a model for execution over time. Collins describes high-performing organizations with functional cultures as possessing the following characteristics with regard to clear performance markers that are:

- self-imposed constraints
- appropriate to the specific enterprise
- largely within the company's control to achieve
- within a proper time frame—long enough to manage, yet short enough to have teeth
- imposed by the organization upon itself
- achieved with high consistency[39]

Functional cultures find ways not only to maintain a long-term view, but also remain nimble and innovative *ahead of* changing market conditions. Apple found a way to embark on a twenty-mile march with self-imposed constraints (i.e., no more than seven products) while continuing to innovate. First introduced in 2015, the Apple Watch was an early entry into the smartwatch market and continues to adapt and thrive in an increasingly crowded market.[40]

Commitment to Change—Pervasive *and* Varied

An important characteristic in functional cultures is a pervasive and certain commitment to change. While every culture has pockets of resistance and recalcitrant naysayers, functional cultures have a critical mass of people and departments committed to change. This does not happen by chance, but rather is the collective result of the other characteristics found in functional cultures coming together to produce this artifact. Additionally, the commitment to change is varied and takes shape in different ways throughout the organization.

At their core, functional cultures are deeply committed to continuous improvement. They have the humble and purpose-driven leadership that values employees and nurtures assertive and positive employee behavior based on clear and adaptable core values. With strategy that has both a short-term focus and long-term view, a general understanding of the dynamic forces shaping the external environment can be found throughout the organization.

The commitment to change may take different forms throughout the organization in functional cultures. For example, academic affairs and student affairs divisions may have a commitment to change that seeks to identify and pursue several new initiatives that connect to national reform efforts like Achieving the Dream and Guided Pathways or Open Educational Resources and Flipped Classrooms.

In contrast, an administrative services division may commit to change through continuous improvement of services in facilities public safety, refinement of processes in human resources and the business office, and technological upgrades in information technology. Similarly, a workforce development division may also commit to change through continual refinement of on-demand program offerings and customized services to local businesses.

Despite the various forms of commitment throughout the college, the resolve to change remains steadfast in functional cultures with the capacity to pursue the right amount of change, in the right ways, to produce positive results. Like any muscle in a living organism, change must be exercised the right amount. The more it is used, the stronger it becomes. The less it is exercised, the more susceptible the muscle is to weakness, atrophy, and dysfunction.

DYSFUNCTIONAL CULTURES

Although all cultures reside somewhere along the spectrum of functional and dysfunctional, few leaders would admit that their college suffers from a dysfunctional culture. However, failure to manage the productive paradox found in functional cultures results in the negative and tangible characteristics found in dysfunctional cultures.

Leadership—Narcissistic

A common contributor to dysfunction in many organizations is the leadership. Whether a leader creates a cult of personality through narcissistic decisions based on self-promotion or a disengaged leader fosters a disconnected culture by only concerning themselves with decisions that may impact their own individual preservation and job security,[41] cultures are more easily turned to dysfunction than they are to more functional characteristics. While many institutions can overcome the tenure of one bad president or a periodic poor senior leader, some colleges suffer from a string of marginal executives that damage the culture over time and make productive transformation even more challenging.

Poor leadership can take root at any level of the organization and impact the culture. Dysfunction at the board level can create tremendous distractions for the college. Board members going "rogue" can create negative press for colleges that takes away from the important work called for in the mission statement. Board-level acrimony can hinder the collective ability of the board to carry out its fiduciary responsibility to steward the resources of the college and place the accreditation of the entire enterprise at risk.[42] Similarly, accreditation can be jeopardized through a board's micromanagement and inability to successfully navigate presidential transitions.[43]

Presidents and senior leaders that lack humility and vulnerability and bring unwavering top-down leadership styles into formal roles can quickly produce dysfunction at all levels. When leaders create distance from their employees, they tend to pay attention to surface items and ignore the essence of issues, resulting in ill-advised decisions.

In addition, informal leadership roles taken by faculty and staff can become dysfunctional and work against the tide of productive results and momentum within an organization. Informal leaders of resistance use their power and influence to maintain the status quo through tactics both overt and seemingly invisible. Younger or newer employees with energy and ideas often choose to operate on the fringes of the organization, quietly going about their creative work in fear of getting noticed by the informal resistance leaders resident in the culture—the great protectors of yesterday and all that was.

Employee Status—Secondary and Unclear

Students are most certainly at the core of every community college—the raison d'etre! However, dysfunctional cultures fail to elevate the importance of employee well-being with student well-being and are often characterized by employees feeling undervalued and entitled to whatever recognition or benefit they do receive. If employees do not feel valued, they are less likely to be invested in the spirit of the daily work, perform to the best of their abilities, anticipate problems, or make quality decisions that contribute to a high-performing organization.

As the Gallup Organization found in their research on the modern global workplace, about one in eight workers are

> psychologically committed to their jobs and likely to be making positive contributions to their organizations. The majority of employees worldwide—63%—are "not engaged," meaning they lack motivation and are less likely to invest discretionary effort in organizational goals or outcomes. And 24% are "actively disengaged," indicating they are unhappy and unproductive at work and liable to spread negativity to coworkers. In rough numbers, this translates into 900 million not engaged and 340 million actively disengaged workers around the globe.[44]

The majority of the global workforce is disengaged, sitting there on the fence, waiting for a spark of inspiration with so much wasted spirit and productivity. It follows then that the majority of the workforce at community colleges across the country is disengaged as well, and that's a major problem for leaders trying to change the culture of their organization.

Factors that can foster dysfunction in the culture and accelerate a lack of employee engagement can include a widespread perception of disparity. If people feel they are being treated differently than others, they can spend as much time in the rumor mill comparing themselves and others as they do in their own work. The perception of management having their "favorites" and "sacred cows" drains the culture of engagement and fosters negative feelings, attitudes, and behaviors. Employees can feel helpless when management creates "untouchable" people or projects regardless of poor performance or progress. Helplessness erodes engagement and, as that deteriorates, individual and collective performance soon follow.

As Peter Block writes, "entitlement is empowerment run aground" and an overbearing sense of entitlement can calcify dysfunction within a culture.[45] It may be misguided union or governance leadership that has lost sight of the big picture, ineffective supervisors who roll over to any challenge and allow entitlement to expand, or small and subtle "gives" by an organization over time, absent any cohesive strategy that keeps the culture aligned in functional ways. Regardless, entitlement is often at the core of most dysfunctional cultures.

Additionally, morale committees or climate surveys that quantify morale at low levels are good indicators that employee recognition often plays an important role in an entrenched culture. When people do not feel recognized for their work, the sense of connection and engagement declines. As a result, dark humor becomes a coping mechanism and breeds contempt for management, other departments, and any place or anyone lacking familiarity and connection.

Engagement can also be put at risk when individuals lose a sense of work/ life balance. Too much work or too much life can alter the impact on the employee, but regardless of the weight, too much of either is not good for the organization. Leaders must think about engagement very intentionally and work with supervisors to consider work/life balance issues, as they are becoming increasingly important to younger employees.

Core Values — Vague

Most often flowing directly from poor leadership, a dysfunctional culture typically fails to adhere to a set of core values, compromises the spirit of the values by justifying bad decisions, or at worst, fails to even have a set of core values. When decisions lack coherency, employees have little context or understanding of why and how decisions are being made. Combined with minimal communication, employees are left to rely on the rumor mill and ad hoc hallway conversations to make sense of the organizational reality, which can change at a moment's notice with whatever decision comes down next from on high.

Core values can influence culture in meaningful ways. Without core values supported by a culture of accountability, employee behavior can vary greatly and work against a cohesive functional culture. If senior leaders fail to espouse the importance of core values like integrity and doing the right thing or modeling the way, they put accountability at risk. Without accountability behaviors defined in all corners of an organization, dysfunction is likely to seep into the culture and erode performance in significant ways. For example, without clear values, different subcultures and departments are left to define their own cultural norms that may be in conflict with one another and accelerate the associated dysfunction with disparate values and expectations that take shape in disconnected subcultures.

Core values can also be inappropriately co-opted to provide rationale for bad decisions. For example, justifying a lack of transparency as maintaining the integrity of a process can result in harboring and withholding information on a regular basis that limits the context for people throughout the organization and fosters uninformed decision-making at all levels. Employees are left to connect the dots themselves, sometimes with dots that do not even exist, by infusing rumor and conjecture into the daily rhythm of the enterprise. Absent meaningful information, coworkers can turn on one another, become suspicious, and consequently raise the level of stress and anxiety while simultaneously lowering the level of productivity and effectiveness.

Perhaps worst of all, a continual adaptation of core values in dysfunctional cultures injects a climate of fear. When people fear for their jobs and their livelihoods, the hallway conversations are not centered on strengthening connections, nurturing relationships, caring for students, or the current projects and priorities of the organization. Instead, people are more concerned about who is in trouble next, who is looking for what job where, or how to create distractions away from a person or department, often increasing the amount of misinformation evident throughout the organization.

A culture with vague core values (or an absence thereof), when combined with unrealistic goals or ambitious self-interest, can experience dysfunction to the point of criminal behavior. For example, the corporate accounting scandal within consumer electronics giant Toshiba is an unfortunate model of how unethical behavior is allowed to persist when a culture has lost its way.

Over a seven-year period, employees overstated profits and misrepresented the financial statements of Toshiba to mislead shareholders. In a somewhat unique case, the employees were not acting on specific directives from executives, but rather responding to unrealistic profit targets set by senior management and finding any means necessary, including illegal and fraudulent, to achieve the desired results.[46] Similarly, the dysfunction found in the organizational cultures of multiple corporations led to financial mismanagement and significant fraud. The scandals of Enron and Arthur Anderson were dwarfed by the culture of secrecy and greed at AGI, Lehman Brothers, Fannie Mae, Freddie Mac, Goldman Sachs, Morgan Stanley, and others that led to the financial collapse and Great Recession.[47]

Similarly, disastrous results from dysfunctional cultures like Toshiba have appeared in higher education as well. From 2005 to 2015, multiple scandals have tarnished the reputations of storied athletic programs for a variety of reasons, all stemming from a lack of core values and transparency. A "culture of reverence" for the prominent football program and coach that led to scandal in the Penn State University football program reflected an insular culture that lacked any form of accountability or transparency.[48]

One of the more prominent cases occurred at the University of North Carolina, where academic fraud was allowed to continue for nearly two decades.[49] Without a commitment to transparency, the widespread reach and influence of culture can lead to unwise decisions that compromise the overall focus and performance organization.

Employee Behavior—Passive-Aggressive

Dysfunctional cultures are plagued by passive-aggressive behaviors that can emerge from reinforcing aspects of culture. At the foundation, passive-aggressive behavior comes from an unclear scope of authority and decision rights, as well as a lack of accountability.[50] When these are present, people find "workarounds" to get things done. They find their "go-to" contact in each office and bypass those with the formal responsibility who fail to deliver.

Another common tactic employees use in dysfunctional cultures is to feign agreement in meetings to pacify leaders and then actively work against whatever was agreed upon to delay, undermine, or even prevent progress from occurring.[51] For example, staff in a registrar's office might meet to talk about streamlining the transcript evaluation process to create capacity that will change the role of the transcript evaluator to include scanning old transcripts into the new imaging system and reduce turnaround time for students. In the strategy meeting, all the staff agree to make this happen. In the subsequent weeks, the transcript evaluator quietly rallies her colleagues to stall and delay changing anything. When timelines aren't met, the supervisor is unable to gather the courage to hold people accountable, so the slow transcript evaluation process remains as is and the new imaging system is used in marginal ways that yield little impact.

Passive-aggressive behavior also appears in dysfunctional cultures where unclear goals and misinformation abound. A lack of clarity in direction combined with misinformation or poor communication gives employees plausible deniability. Similarly, excessive top-down directives consistently given over time can enable a sense of learned helplessness among employees, thwarting initiative and resulting in employees defaulting to an unproductive pattern of *"just tell me what to do and I'll do it."*

Fear seeps deep into the organization and people begin to make decisions by avoiding punishment. If something goes wrong, quick and extensive finger-pointing surfaces from all angles in attempt to both find and elude blame. Passive-aggressive behavior appears in all cultures, but dysfunctional ones are unable to minimize it and suffer the consequences.

Strategy—Reactionary

Dysfunction also appears in cultures that are unable to balance the paradox of staying focused on short-term goals and issues while simultaneously taking a long-term view. Leaders in dysfunctional cultures often create what can be called *"strategy du jour . . .* when executives consistently overreact to a single data point and take the entire organization in a new direction on a frequent basis. Often the result of hallway or ad hoc meetings in obscure places and making decisions in the absence of those who are actually responsible for that sort of thing."[52] This reactionary behavior takes a toll on the culture and is not sustainable over time.

When problems are not dealt with in a direct and consistent manner, they are either ignored, transferred, or just "made to go away" so as not to bother the leaders who are responsible. This lack of accountability can hinder an organization in the long term. As a result, today's problems become tomorrow's crises.

For example, a local agency with a marginal reputation may approach a college with an exciting partnership possibility that involves some level of risk that is not taken into account. The partnership is announced with great fanfare and compelling headlines that are celebrated by all involved. After a brief period of time, the shadow side of the agency's reputation plays out and the partnership collapses. The public distrust in the college created by the subsequent negative headlines far outweigh the brief and flashy positive headlines gleaned from the original announcement.

When decisions are made without a clear strategy, people find it difficult to put their daily work in perspective and align their efforts with some larger direction of the organization. With no accounting for the long term, short-term decisions can appear contradictory and create confusion within the culture. Staff experience a mild form of post-traumatic stress syndrome from the shocking experience of having their professional lives turned upside down by leaders who make decisions in the moment absent any meaningful plan or coherent strategy.

Leaders in dysfunctional cultures make the case that the college needs to be entrepreneurial or proactive to take advantage of opportunities that arise. With minimal checks and balances absent a balance of short- and long-term strategy, dysfunctional cultures blindly pursue doomed strategies.

For example, multiple cases exist of presidents spearheading the development of new buildings, programs, or theaters under the auspices of "adding to the quality of life in the community" when there was marginal, or worse yet, no real market demand or proven financial plan. The programs consume unnecessary resources, stretch organizational capacity, and wither on the vine when the president leaves. These critical and expensive distractions only happen in dysfunctional cultures that are prone to reactionary strategy.

The short-term focus modeled by some leaders can easily filter down throughout the organization. Decisions are made with regard to purchases, facilities, student success and other areas of the operation that save money or frustration in the short term but create major problems in the future. Guarding against reactionary strategy and effectively balancing the paradox of strategy is essential for avoiding dysfunction in organizational cultures.

Commitment to Change—Isolated

Cultures paralyzed by dysfunction are too disconnected and distracted to cultivate a meaningful and pervasive commitment to change. If any commitment does exist, it is isolated within individual employees and departments. This isolation is not the result of intentional actions on the part of leaders, but rather a combination of purposeful actions among employees in the presence of several key factors.

Similar to the manner in which the other attributes come together to create a commitment to change in functional cultures, the same attributes coalesce to create the opposite effect in dysfunctional cultures. Leadership that is narcissistic and allows for vague core values facilitates learned helplessness among employees and empowers resistance to change within subcultures throughout the organization. Additionally, when the pervasive organizational strategy is reactionary, employees are left to wait for the next directive to come from the top. This dynamic increases the resistance to change as the organization shifts into survival mode to simply endure the next shock to the system of whatever reactionary strategy is employed next.

Consider the case of a new workforce development director who follows a long-term strategy to transform the corporate training function at a college. After an eighteen-month period of managing difficult staff transitions and daily rewiring of new systems and behaviors, things are looking up. During the same period, she has carefully and slowly cultivated a working relationship with the senior vice president of a large employer who has a history of meeting workforce training needs through internal capacity. Things finally come together to make a move that is likely to be a harbinger of real change and a new day for corporate training at the college.

Just when she prepares to put forth a large training proposal, the president becomes aware and calls everything off because an influential board member owns a company who competes with the large employer. The proposal gets shelved, the relationship with the employer evaporates, the momentum for change in the department stalls, and the workforce development director becomes unsure of how to pursue partnerships in the future if thoughtful strategy can be erased by reactionary tactics. The director shuts down, resorts to a "just tell me what to do boss" mentality, and updates her resume.

The absence of a noticeable commitment to change evident in dysfunctional cultures influences morale, relationships, image, and performance. The isolated areas where a commitment does exist are usually short-lived and dependent upon individuals that will likely seek other institutions in hopes of finding a more vibrant and functional organization. Meanwhile, those employees committed to resisting change are left to reinforce their strongholds for the status quo while they wait for the culture to reject change enough to prompt yet another round of turnover in the senior administration of the college.

CONCLUDING THOUGHTS

Culture is the most pervasive element of an organization and is reflected in the people, the facilities, the programs, services, structures, and systems. At a time when community colleges face increasingly complex demands for student access and completion, doing more *and better* with less, and anticipating environmental shifts in their environment, culture often surfaces as a barrier to change. Managing the paradoxical nature of the attributes in functional cultures separates organizations from those with dysfunctional ones. The remaining chapters of this book will explore the dynamics associated with the key characteristics of cultural paradox that can help drive change and create functional, high-performing cultures.

NOTES

1. London, H. B. (1978). *The Culture of a Community College*. New York: Praeger Publishers.
2. Cameron, K. S., and Quinn, R. E. (2011). *Diagnosing and Changing Organizational Culture: Based on the Competing Values Framework*. San Francisco: Jossey-Bass, 13.
3. Connors, R., and Smith, T. (2012). *Change the Culture, Change the Game*. New York: Portfolio/Penguin.
4. Watkins, M. D. (2013). "What Is Organizational Culture and Why Should We Care?" *Harvard Business Review*. May 15, 2013. 1–5.
5. Schein, E. H. (1985). *Organizational Culture and Leadership: A Dynamic View*. San Francisco: Jossey-Bass, 12.
6. Kempner, Ken. (1991). "Understanding Cultural Conflict." In *Culture and Ideology in Higher Education: Advancing a Critical Agenda*, W. G. Tierney (ed). New York: Praeger. 131.
7. Ibid.
8. Ibid.
9. Cameron, K. S., and Ettington, D. R. (1988). "The Conceptual Foundations of Organizational Culture." In *Higher Education: Handbook of Theory and Research*, vol. 4, J. C. Smart (ed.). New York: Agathon Press, 356–96.
10. Kuh, G. D., and Whitt, E. J. (1988). *The Invisible Tapestry: Culture in American Colleges and Universities*. ASHE-ERIC Higher Education Report No. 1. Washington, DC: ASHE, iii.
11. Tierney, W. G. (1991). *Organizational Culture in Higher Education: Defining the Essentials*. In *Organizations and Governance in Higher Education: An ASHE Reader*, M. W. Peterson, E. E. Chaffee, and T. H. White (eds.). Needham Heights, MA: Ginn Press.
12. Cameron and Quinn. (2011). *Diagnosing and Changing Organizational Culture: Based on the Competing Values Framework*.
13. Cameron and Ettington. (1988). "The Conceptual Foundations of Organizational Culture."
14. Cameron and Quinn. (2011). *Diagnosing and Changing Organizational Culture: Based on the Competing Values Framework*.
15. Lorsch, J. W., and McTague, E. (2016). "Culture Is Not the Culprit." *Harvard Business Review*. April, 2016. 1.
16. Sturt, D., and Nordstrom, T. (2015). "4 Stories Great Leaders Tell to Engage Their People." *Forbes Magazine*. January 22, 2015. http://www.forbes.com/sites/davidsturt/2015/01/22/4-stories-great-leaders-tell-to-engage-their-people/#3ffb10fd648e.
17. Ibid.
18. Dweck, C. (2012). *Mindset*. New York: Ballantine Books.

19. Meyerson, D. (2001). "Radical Change, the Quiet Way." *Harvard Business Review* 79 (9), October, 2001, 100.

20. Weick, K. E. (1976). "Educational Organizations as Loosely Coupled Systems." *Administrative Science Quarterly* 21 (1), March, 1976. 1–19.

21. Linder, V., and Alfred, R. L. (1990). *Rhetoric to Reality: Managing Paradox.* Ann Arbor, MI: Community College Consortium.

22. Sydow, D., and Alfred, R. L. (2013). *Re-visioning Community Colleges.* Lanham, MD: Rowman & Littlefield.

23. Zogby, J. (2007). *The Way We'll Be.* New York: Random House.

24. Sheridan, R. (2013). *Joy, Inc.* New York: Penguin Group. 147.

25. Brown, B. (2010). *The Power of Vulnerability.* TED Houston. 2010. https://www.youtube.com/watch?v=iCvmsMzlF7o (website accessed October 14, 2017).

26. Collins, J. (2001). *Good to Great.* New York: HarperCollins, 33.

27. Mackey, J., and Sisodia, R. (2014). *Conscious Capitalism.* Boston: Harvard Business Review Press. 189.

28. Ibid., 75.

29. Spiegelman, P. (2011). "Deliver Value to Your Employees—Your Most Important Stakeholders." *Inc.com.* July, 2011. http://www.inc.com/articles/201107/beryl-companies-paul-spiegelman-deliver-value-to-employees-your-most-important-stakeholders.html.

30. Cameron, K., Mora, C., Leutscher, T., and Calarco, M. (2011). "Effects of Positive Practices on Organizational Effectiveness." *The Journal of Applied Behavioral Science* 47 (3), 271. Thousand Oaks: Sage.

31. Mann, A., and Dvorak, N. (2016). "Employee Recognition: Low Cost, High Impact." *Gallup News: Business Journal.* June 28, 2016. http://www.gallup.com/businessjournal/193238/employee-recognition-low-cost-high-impact.aspx?g_source=EMPLOYEE_ENGAGEMENT&g_medium=topic&g_campaign=tiles.

32. Sisodia, R., Sheth, J., and Wolfe, D. B. (2007). *Firms of Endearment.* Upper Saddle River, NJ: Wharton School Publishing.

33. Sinek, S. (2009). *Start with Why: How Great Leaders Inspire Everyone to Action.* New York: Penguin Group.

34. Sisodia, Sheth, and Wolfe. (2007). *Firms of Endearment.*

35. http://disneyatwork.com/disneys-four-keys-to-a-great-guest-experience/. Website accessed October 25, 2017.

36. Sisodia, Sheth, and Wolfe. (2007). *Firms of Endearment.*

37. Sisodia, R., Sheth, J., Wolfe, D.B. (2007). *Firms of Endearment.* Upper Saddle River, NJ: Wharton School Publishing.

38. Collins, J. (2010). *Great by Choice.* New York: HarperCollins. 65.

39. Ibid.

40. Pierce, D. (2015). "iPhone Killer: The Secret History of the Apple Watch." Wired.com. April, 2015. https://www.wired.com/2015/04/the-apple-watch/.

41. Chamorro-Premuzic, T. (2016). "Why We Keep Hiring Narcissistic CEOs." *Harvard Business Review.* November 29, 2016.

42. Berman, C., St. Clair, S., and Cohen, J. (2015). "College of DuPage Trustees Work Amid Serious Dysfunction." *Chicago Tribune.* October 19, 2015.

43. Smith, S. (2015). "A Three-Year Search." *Inside Higher Education.* June 17, 2015. https://www.insidehighered.com/news/2015/06/17/tension-between-faculty-and-administration-impacts-nassau-community-colleges (accessed December 11, 2016).

44. Crabtree, S. (2013). "Worldwide, 13% of Employees Are Engaged at Work." *Gallup News.* October 8, 2013. http://www.gallup.com/poll/165269/worldwide-employees-engaged-work.aspx.

45. Block, P. (1993). *Stewardship.* San Francisco: Berrett-Koehler, 34.

46. Fukase, A. (2015). "Toshiba Accounting Scandal Draws Record Fine from Regulators." *Wall Street Journal.* December 7, 2015.

47. Lenzer, R. (2012). "The 2008 Meltdown and Where the Blame Falls." *Forbes.com.* June 2, 2012. http://www.forbes.com/sites/robertlenzner/2012/06/02/the-2008-meltdown-and-where-the-blame-falls/#30e800666fd0

48. Wolverton, B. (2012). "Penn State's Culture of Reverence Led to 'Total Disregard' for Children's Safety." *Chronicle of Higher Education.* July 12, 2012. http://www.chronicle.com/article/Penn-States-Culture-of/132853.

49. Ganim, S., and Sayers, D. (2014). "UNC Report Finds 18 Years of Academic Fraud to Keep Athletes Playing." *CNN.* October 23, 2014. http://www.cnn.com/2014/10/22/us/unc-report-academic-fraud/

50. Neilson, G. L., Pasternack, B. A., and Van Nuys, K. E. (2005). "The Passive-Aggressive Organization." *Harvard Business Review* 83 (10), October, 2005. 82–92.

51. Ibid.

52. Tobak, S. (2012). "7 Signs of a Dysfunctional Company." *CBS News: MoneyWatch.* February 2, 2012. http://www.cbsnews.com/news/7-signs-of-a-dysfunctional-company/.

Chapter Two

Transformation

Where Does Culture Fit?

Cultural adaptation to any major change takes courage, conviction, and discipline based upon a sense of urgency in order to remain relevant. It must be advanced by design, not circumstance or happenstance, and at a pace designed to ensure the long-term success of the organization.
—Dan Phelan, President, Jackson College

"The frightening uncertainty that traditionally accompanied major organizational change has been superseded by the frightening uncertainty now associated with staying the same."[1] In this quote, Cameron and Quinn capture the essence of community colleges' greatest challenge today. How do leaders transform their institutions if culture is inherently wired to keep things the same? Culture reflects the past and present of an organization and it has a significant impact on their long-term success as well.[2] If leaders can shape, if not transform, organizational culture, they can do the same with the future of the organization.

Transforming organizational culture does not happen overnight. Culture develops over time, which requires a focused and intentional process for evolving, leading to observed change. Community colleges are remarkably similar, but different at the same time. Across the nation, the same taglines are plastered on community college websites and advertising billboards:

- "education that works,"
- "transforming lives,"
- "start here go anywhere,"
- "your future starts now,"
- "your community's college," and

31

• "where learning is for life."

While these taglines reflect similarity in the important *work* of community colleges, the *cultures* within these organizations reflect great variation. They move at their own pace, with their own nuances and, although fundamental elements of organizational culture reside in each college, no single formula exists to transform culture. A prescription cannot be written to move a culture from point A to point B. As the environment changes, there exists no standard procedure or process to adapt the culture of an organization to the new realities.[3]

Cultural transformation requires great intention to pursue an action agenda of renewal and inculcate the behaviors and processes within the organization to make it continuous.[4] Fixed mind-sets and inflated memories of the past can inhibit organizational culture and make any efforts to change culture short-lived and unsuccessful. Many times the general success of a college sends positive reinforcing signals throughout the culture, to the point that change becomes harder and harder as barriers to meaningful, transformative change continue to build.

Inertia can increase over time, even in successful organizations. It can create a malaise that slowly encompasses the entire operation, turns the organizational focus inward, and compromises overall performance. As Jim Collins said, "Good is the enemy of great."[5] His research outlines the philosophical elements for leaders to consider breaking through the seemingly impenetrable wall of organizational culture to move an institution from resting on its laurels to embracing a strategic and ongoing change agenda.

Moving an organization from good to great requires effective leadership that Collins describes as Level 5 leadership. He goes on to outline increasing organizational performance as getting the right people in the right positions within the organization, surfacing and confronting the brutal facts, developing a simple and coherent message for change to focus the organization, reinforcing disciplined thought and action throughout the organization, leveraging technology wherever possible, and creating a sense of momentum to inspire forward-thinking and change-oriented behaviors to keep the culture evolving with the times.[6]

Case studies documenting the elements that comprise cultural transitions and eventual transformation reveal the slow-moving nature of deep cultural change and highlight the personal attributes of leaders—particularly focused vigilance, and the ability to manage the paradox of patience and speed that are effective in managing change. Like the great UCLA men's basketball coach, John Wooden, told his players, "Be quick, but don't hurry."[7]

The following three case studies demonstrate how organizations can be transformed through intentional actions to shape and evolve organizational culture over time. Each case brings different elements of the *Good to Great* framework to life under varied circumstances. Each person interviewed for these case studies was quick to point out that the college is not perfect by any stretch of the imagination, nor did they single-handedly made the difference. Like the Level 5 leaders Collins describes, they looked in the mirror when things did not go well and they looked out the window when things went well. They essentially put the wheels in motion and tended to the culture so others could develop, lead, and thrive.

THE VISION THING:
CENTRAL PIEDMONT COMMUNITY COLLEGE

I met Tony Zeiss about fifteen years ago when I was president of the National Council of Instructional Administrators and he was the keynote speaker at our annual conference. I asked him how, as president, he walked the line between staying out of the weeds and knowing what was going on in the college. Without missing a beat, he responded that he only concerned himself when the issues involved one or more of three things: resources, the brand, and the quality of programs and services. I walked away thinking I had my three guiding principles for a future presidency and then quickly realized a president could use any one of those three principles to involve themselves with any situation, underscoring the strategic discretion a leader must employ to touch culture in the right ways at the right time.

When Tony Zeiss arrived at Central Piedmont Community College (CPCC) in December of 1992, the college had experienced three decades of success. The very success that defined its past, however, was gradually getting in the way of the college's future. As a founding member of the League of Innovation, CPCC long considered itself an innovative college. The college had been nationally recognized twelve years earlier, and employees were quick to tell the new president how important that award was to them. It was increasingly clear to see that the general behaviors and attitudes were influenced by people resting on their laurels, which seemed to be clouding the forward-thinking vision of the institution.

CPCC had a very strong sense of mission to serve students, but the vision was unclear. No facilities or academic master plan existed. The presidential search took more than a year, and, instead of appointing a single interim president, the board had the three vice presidents handling the presidential responsibilities on a rotating basis. As the college finished its self-study process for accreditation the following year, it received forty-four "must change" statements from the Southern Accreditation Commission of Schools (SACS).[8]

Developing the Workforce and Community

It became evident that the workforce development focus from the early years of the college had been diminished with an increased focus on the liberal arts during the 1980s. Consequently, the organizational culture had grown more internally focused and had not continued to strengthen and evolve the community engagement it once had. With that conceptual foundation defined and the mandate for change from the accreditation results, Dick Alfred and Pat Carter were hired as consultants to facilitate the development of a master plan process. A total of thirty-four internal and thirty-seven external forums were held to create a vision that resulted in identifying the intent to become the nation's leader in workforce development.

This sent a strong signal to the liberal arts faculty that the college needed to reexamine its priorities around employees, students, and community. The president broke things down to two key questions for decision-making throughout the culture. As Dr. Zeiss shared, "With every decision, people need to ask,'Is it good for students?' and 'Is it good for the community?' If the answer to both are 'yes,' then it's safe to say that it will be good for the college."[9] Together with the new vision, these questions were the foundation to drive the culture to be more service oriented and better serve students and the community.

A Bold Plan

The new energy and focus began to drive change at multiple levels within the organization. A few key retirements and separations helped rearrange staffing patterns and organizational structure to create new capacity. However, the changes did not come without a cost. A new vision, new plans calling for the creation of new campuses throughout Mecklenburg County, and a renewed focus on technical education were more change than some were willing to pursue, given that the college had been nationally recognized twelve years earlier.

Angst and consternation grew in pockets throughout the college. Former employees started getting their opinions heard through negative stories in the local media. One dean paid for a protester to walk around campus and campaign against the changes taking place. The president stayed on message with the local media that "change is hard" and went about holding a number of open forums to allow faculty and staff the opportunity to vent and learn more about the changes.

Change and Challenge

Two former employees filed lawsuits that the college eventually won during a two-year period of litigation. Along the way, leaders from the Christian faith community brought a petition with 15,000 signatures to the president demanding the individuals be reinstated. When four of the preachers came to his office, the president, in an effort to thwart any wayward actions in the exchange, set up a fifth chair that remained empty. He told the preachers that the chair was for Jesus, who of course would want the conversation to remain noble and of good will and intent. He spent the next several months going to every community event possible to continue gaining their trust and support. [10]

Although this was his second presidency, he accelerated his personal reading on the subject of organizational change. During these early years of his time at CPCC, he came to focus on four key steps to initiate fundamental cultural change: (1) Engage the stakeholders, (2) State the organization's problem or need to change and create some anxiety, (3) Quickly paint a vision to solve the problem or adopt needed changes, (4) Finally, tie the change(s) to an existing core value of the college. In this case, by tying change to a core value like innovation (amplifying CPCC's pride in the League of Innovation legacy), the idea of change seemed more evolutionary and less threatening than something imposed with revolutionary disruption.

A Multicampus College

With the master plans in place for facilities and academic programs, money was raised through successful bond issues and the first branch campus was established in 1996. Over the next eight years, five more campuses would follow. While the new campuses brought great excitement, there was also great concern. The organizational structure had to be changed to accommodate the new operations of the college. Critical decisions had to be made: Would the campuses compete against one another with campus presidents decentralized inside a single district? Or would the campuses be led by deans who were part of a more centralized cohesive "one-college" philosophy? After examining other multicampus community college environments, the choice was made to go with a single college/branch campus structure.

Fears about the staffing pattern were tempered with existing academic deans being reassigned to the various campuses. Faculty and staff were given the option to be reassigned to new campuses located closer to their homes where they knew the local community, schools, and neighborhoods. This approach sent an important message to employees that their personal lives and preferences were important and valued. Additional concerns about branch campuses pulling enrollment away from the main campus were alleviated over the next decade, as the main campus enrollment actually grew and continues to do so to this day.

External Forces

When the recession of 2001 and the Great Recession of 2008 occurred, the workforce development focus was placed front and center for the college. The workforce retraining demands were significant and called for dramatic changes to occur. After years of operating at a deficit, the workforce development function transformed itself into a profit center.

Challenges with public funding intensified and required changes within the college. Although the local bonding supported the aggressive capital expansions, the state support for operating did not keep pace. In 1992, base operating aid from the state represented 72 percent of the operating budget. Those resources went on a steady decline over the next twenty-five years, eventually representing 44 percent of the budget. Rather than implementing across-the-board budget cuts and implementing travel and hiring freezes, a growth mind-set of abundance helped develop a far different approach.

Entrepreneurship and Innovation

Building on the core value of innovation at the college, a new core value of entrepreneurship was added. The college invested to increase the capacity in grants administration to expand revenues through more aggressive grant writing. Today, CPCC receives nearly $25 million annually in grants and secures roughly 90 percent of all grants for which it applies. Fundraising was greatly expanded as well with the CPCC Foundation endowment growing from roughly $3 million in 1992 to roughly $35 million in 2018.

The flexibility found in alternative revenue streams allowed the college to develop creative programs such as the Opportunity Scholars Program. In partnership with five local high schools, who are all Title I schools, private dollars have been raised to provide a full-tuition scholarship and computer for any high school graduate with the ability to benefit. In addition, the students must work with an assigned mentor and enroll in a high-demand major. A similar program track is being developed for the parents of these students.

To advance the new core value of entrepreneurship, a separate 501(c)3 organization was established to bring additional revenue into the college. Created as the CPCC Services Corporation, this auxiliary entity is guided by the President's Entrepreneurship Team (PET), which is comprised of thirty-three faculty and staff whose sole purpose is to identify and develop ideas to create revenue streams for the college.

With three-year terms (one-third turning over annually), PET members attend four meetings a year; are required to bring one idea to every meeting; and provide feedback to evaluate all the ideas brought forward. As ideas are developed and pursued, 15 percent of any profit goes to the idea owner; 20

percent to their department; and 65 percent into the fund balance to support future ventures. Since its founding in 2001, the CPCC Services Corporation has grown the fund balance to $4.5 million.

The premise behind the new 501(c)3 organization was to tap into the intellectual capital and awaken the entrepreneurial spirit within the college culture. Two great examples of ideas turned into successful ventures include a television program focused on supporting the needs of English language learners and a research institute. The television program quickly grew and was licensed in communities across twenty-nine states and later sold to the McGraw-Hill publishing company. The revenue generated from the sale was distributed as described earlier. The Research Institute was initially established to complement the increased grant activity at the college, but later grew into a multifaceted operation with regional and national contracts to support the staff payroll—independent of the college's operating budget.

Transformation

Eleanor Roosevelt said, "It's better to light a candle than curse the darkness." Over a twenty-five-year period, as the external environment became increasingly complex and dark, Central Piedmont Community lit a candle and pursued a path of cultural transformation. Engaging the community to develop a bold master plan created ten successful construction bond referendums (nearly $600 million) over the twenty-five years and expanded the college from one to seven campuses.

These developments fundamentally changed the organizational profile. Key characteristics of the organizational culture like leadership, structure, governance, systems, processes, programs, and services were all dramatically altered through a consistent application of centering the individual and collective decision-making focus of the college squarely on students and the community. Student and employee demographics changed as the college became more integrated into the community.

Workforce development efforts were expanded exponentially, along with grants, alternative revenues, and entrepreneurial ventures. In the end, CPCC transformed its culture from risking the loss of its innovative ways to securing an entrepreneurial spirit that is deeply engrained throughout the organization to forge a successful path into an ever-changing future environment.

GET THE FUNDAMENTALS RIGHT AND THE REST WILL FOLLOW: NORTHERN ESSEX COMMUNITY COLLEGE

I met David Hartleb at a conference in Vail, Colorado, when I was twenty-six years old and working on my doctorate at the University of Michigan. At the time, he was vice president and Provost for Access and Outreach at the

University of Cincinnati, and I asked him what was the most important thing he had learned about leadership. He thought a minute and went on to tell me how delicate the balance was between creating a sense of urgency while remaining patient, a fascinating paradox that is likely the burden of any leader interested in transforming culture.

Throughout the search process in 1996 that brought David Hartleb to be the new president at Northern Essex Community College (NECC), everyone put on a happy face. Board members, faculty, staff, and administrators all seemed to get along just fine and presented a healthy organizational front.[11] Upon his arrival, however, the new president began to reveal a number of issues that failed to surface during the search process.

The former president ruled by a command-and-control method of leadership, having been known to address his displeasure with individuals in front of others. The five-member Cabinet leadership team had all been in place for twenty to thirty years and seemed to get along, although the dynamic was very individualistic and competitive. This allowed the former president to be overly involved in decision-making at the college. As the new president was told, "Cabinet was like having five lions in a cage constantly fighting over the raw meat."[12]

With a strong faculty union and top-down management, there was little space for collaborative governance. As a faculty union leader put it, "Administration creates the initiatives and faculty tell them what's wrong."[13] The majority of the systems, policies, procedures, and practices seemed primarily designed for the employees and not the students. As a result, enrollment declined 25 percent in the year prior to and the year after the new president's arrival.

Board members were in general denial and not interested in hearing about any dysfunction; they were proud of their school. It was indeed clear, however, that despite some fundamental issues, students were being taught by excellent faculty who took pride in delivering an excellent education inside the classroom.

Building Trust and Credibility

Faced with issues to address in almost every corner of the college, the new president set out to build trust and credibility. He did not originally think about transforming the culture, but rather focused on getting the fundamental operations right. Throughout the first six months, the new president had extensive conversations with his Cabinet members, including a retreat that surfaced central differences between his approach to what and how change needed to occur and that of his senior team.

A great example of how desperately change was needed: the vice president for Student Services recommended a Noel-Levitz consultant be brought in to analyze enrollment and student services. The consultant made 167 recommendations for change—167! Within the first eighteen months, Dr. Hartleb built the case for transitions to gain support from his Board of Trustees and replaced all five members of the Cabinet.

With new leadership in place, the organizational focus turned toward the fundamentals, tending to practices, policies, procedures, and systems to make the college more student friendly. The 167 recommendations were prioritized and implemented to the extent possible. Academic systems needed to be analyzed and refined to create more consistency across the multiple divisions. Despite progress in critical areas, the college still lacked a strategic plan that could guide and coordinate activity to advance the organization even further.

Activating Governance for Planning

The governance system was a logical mechanism to employ for the development of a meaningful strategic plan. However, given the polarized norms between faculty and administration that had developed over decades, the governance system needed attention. The core of governance at the college was the All-College Council, comprised of all employees who were welcome to attend the meetings. An Executive Committee was elected with carefully crafted representative slots for various employee groups and divisions. The timing was ripe to actively engage the All-College Council Executive Committee in new and different ways.

About eighteen months into his tenure, the president approached the Executive Committee about playing a central role in the development of the new strategic plan. He provided them a description of a few different consultants and asked them to make their selection for help in facilitating the process. The committee made their choice and the consultants conducted thirty-six focus groups in three days. The consultants, having worked with nearly one hundred community colleges in more than thirty states, told the president, "This is the most dysfunctional college we've ever worked with."[14]

Through monthly visits over the next sixteen months, the consultants worked with the All-College Council Executive Committee to develop priorities, goals, objectives, and strategies for the new strategic plan. Executive Committee members initially resisted presenting the plan to their peers; that was "not their job." But when they acquiesced and presented the plan, it was a powerful cultural artifact that may not have been clear to everyone at the time, but later would prove to light the way for what would become fundamental cultural transformation.[15]

The new strategic plan had eight goals and was really more operational than strategic. However, it brought focus to the collective work of the institution, addressed changes to the fundamental operations of the college, and was finished in three years—two years ahead of the original timeline.

With progress being made on the operational fundamentals, a mechanism was needed to address the insularity of the culture. Most of the employees had been hired from the immediate area and little support had been given for professional travel or encouragement to explore best practices at other institutions. When the college joined the Strategic Horizon Network (SHN), a small group of faculty and staff became the primary participants in the SHN colloquia that were held in June and October of each year.

The design principles for the SHN included each network member college bringing teams of faculty and staff to colloquia that were focused on future trends and strategic thinking happening in industries outside of higher education. Speakers and site visits comprised the essence of the programs that provided participants exposure to issues in healthcare, hospitality and tourism, manufacturing, food service, retail, airlines and transportation, and secondary education. The colloquia provided common learning through uncommon experiences and opened the organizational aperture to view the world in new ways that stretched the collective thinking of the college. Over the years, these experiences built a critical mass of leaders for the array of critical initiatives that would come to shape the culture.

Process Management and Change

From the SHN experiences, a consultant was identified to create competency and capacity throughout the college in the area of process management. Through extensive trainings based in continuous total-quality management, structures and processes were created to continue improving the fundamental operations of the college. A steering committee was formed to receive ideas from faculty and staff for ways to improve processes. The committee would choose three to five priorities each semester for systems that should be improved. Workgroups would then collect and analyze data before making their recommendations to the steering committee.

An important element of this effort that signaled a shift in culture was that the president, to demonstrate his belief and trust in the process, committed to implementing the recommendations to the extent the college budget could afford it. He would not otherwise arbitrarily block the recommendations. The productive and meaningful work of these workgroups created a clear and transparent process that began to change the organization for the better.

Initially, staff were more excited about the new process management efforts than faculty. A tipping point came when a recommendation was made to improve student success rates in developmental math classes. After some early resistance, the faculty pursued this recommendation with successful results. The experience prompted an important minority of faculty to engage in process management at the college.

With more and more faculty supporting the efforts, a sense of energy started to really build around improving processes and a feeling of momentum began to take shape after four or five years. It was years—not months. With deep change gaining traction in the culture, "People started to see that there was value in examining problems using consistent and rational procedures and data. This was really the precursor to joining the Achieving the Dream Network."[16]

Change Accelerators

Getting the flywheel of change in motion for an organization is critically important.[17] Another major lever to help turn that flywheel of change faster toward the feeling of breakthrough was the college's participation in the Achieving the Dream Network (ATD). With one of the early state policy teams working with ATD and through a competitive process, Massachusetts selected NECC as one of four community colleges in the state to join the ATD Network in 2007.[18]

This development provided NECC the opportunity to accelerate its process management work and begin using data in more sophisticated ways. As the culture became even more comfortable with the use of data to surface issues and inform solutions, things began to change. Over time, research and data were increasingly used to support their ideas, requests, or initiatives, which changed the nature of conversations and decision-making at the college.

To address the dysfunction in the interpersonal dynamics of the culture, Appreciative Inquiry (AI) was introduced. AI is an approach to collaborative change that centers on unconditionally positive interactions, perspectives, and ways of problem-solving.[19] This cultural change effort came about from yet another SHN experience where key staff gained exposure around the same time that a new chief academic officer was hired who happened to be a certified AI trainer and facilitator.

The college created a train-the-trainer model to make three different AI trainers available on staff and accelerate the adoption of AI techniques in a variety of ways in different departments. AI became so integrated into the culture at NECC that when the All-College Council engaged in the updating of the strategic plan, it seemed natural to utilize AI methods to develop the goals and strategies. More than three hundred faculty, staff, students, and community members participated in a multiday, off-site charrette, using AI techniques, to explore what was working well at NECC; identify what it looked like when NECC was at its best; and pursue strategies to do more of what worked in the future.

The introduction of the National Coalition Building Institute (NCBI) created an additional lever for cultural change at the college. NCBI was supported by the faculty, staff, and organizational development office, which had been created early on in the new president's tenure. By elevating a talented part-time coordinator and reassigning the office from the Vice President for Administrative Services to become a direct report of the president with support staff, the office played a critical role in new initiatives like NCBI.

The coordinator introduced NCBI to the college and eventually had ten trained NCBI facilitators to help faculty, staff, and students explore issues of gender, race, and culture to find common ground and interests to accelerate problem-solving and produce more meaningful results throughout the organization.

Taken together, AI and NCBI provided complementary resources to inculcate more productive behaviors based on a common conceptual framework, philosophy, and set of tools for faculty and staff. These cultural levers acted together to fundamentally change the daily interactions faculty and staff had with one another—and with students—to focus on more civil, positive, and mutually reinforcing exchanges and shared experiences.

Transformation

The results of these efforts flowed from the creation and use of key levers. Replacing the Cabinet members in the first eighteen months brought new energy and focus to the senior leadership of the culture. Utilizing the governance system to develop a new strategic plan built trust and transparency to the decision-making process. Participation in the Strategic Horizon Network created a small guiding coalition of change agents that opened the culture up to best practices and created a more future-focused orientation that spurred innovation and risk.

The capacity-building efforts for process-change management refined systems that changed behavior in significant ways and in important places at the college. And finally, the combination of Appreciative Inquiry and the National Coalition of Building Institute tools and techniques provided new and more positive approaches toward interpersonal connections, interactions, and relationships that had transformative effects on the culture of the entire college.

Over this fifteen-year period, the culture at Northern Essex Community College went from a divisive and antagonistic culture, characterized by incongruent systems that favored employees over students, to a data-informed, appreciative, and dynamic culture with systems and processes focused on students. Tangible results could be seen through meaningful outcomes and changes in key areas. NECC quickly became an ATD leader school.

The Lawrence branch campus was transformed from being a small extension center to a robust and vibrant branch campus with dynamic community partnerships serving many vulnerable populations—primarily Latino—that resulted in the NECC's being designated as a Hispanic-serving institution. With a more adaptive, outward-facing organizational culture, community partnerships led to increased fundraising that grew the endowment from $76,000 in 1996 to more than $15 million in 2011. And the enrollment troubles were remedied with student enrollment growing 42 percent (5,200 to 7,400 head count) during this period.

AMPLIFYING COMMUNITY:
LORAIN COUNTY COMMUNITY COLLEGE

Having known Roy Church for twenty-five years, I asked him a few years ago what his secret was to staying so energized and engaged. He said he took things one strategic plan at a time. If he was not as excited about the next strategic plan as he was for the last one, he would resign. That thought has always stayed with me, as I think about how presidents can overstay their welcome by unintentionally finding their own level of comfort and invisibly reinforcing a level of ease and familiarity within the organizational culture. It's a critical variable that each president and leader needs to monitor on a regular basis.

Leaving the sunny skies of Florida for the Rust Belt and dormant smokestacks in suburban Cleveland in 1987, Roy Church took the reins as president of Lorain County Community College (LCCC) to be part of not just an awakening at the college, but also a turnaround story for the entire community. It certainly was not an overnight success, but rather a slow and steady transformational success. He retired from LCCC twenty-nine years after he'd arrived.

During the economic recession from 1980 to 1983, Lorain County had nearly 25 percent unemployment and more than eighty local businesses went completely out of business. By 1987, the community was looking to leverage every resource possible to change the fortunes and the attitudes of the community. The Board of Trustees at LCCC saw the opportunity to hire a new president as a chance to position the college as a major resource in the rebirth of the region. After an uneven start with the founding president, followed by an interim president, and an uncomfortable separation from the second president after a fifteen-year tenure, and another interim president, the stage was set for the third permanent president.

The previous fourteen years saw the college develop solid systems and infrastructure, but the last few years of the prior president's tenure were not as active as his first several, and, as a few board members put it, "LCCC was a solid institution that was coasting."[20] The college had grown quite insular and occasionally referenced the community, but seemed to be working off of old data and assumptions without actively engaging the community or managing meaningful contacts and networks. During the interview process, Roy asked for, but never received, any form of strategic planning documents. He received an annual plan and budget, which were useful, but no meaningful sense of strategic planning existed.

Looking for Levers

For most of the first two years on the job, the new president concentrated his efforts on understanding the culture: what worked well, how did power and energy flow through the organization, what was behind the insularity, and what might be good levers for change. He affirmed that the programs and services were generally good but lacked future-orientation or external focus. Stereotypical divisions existed between faculty and administration and liberal arts and technical faculty, and support staff generally felt disconnected and underappreciated.

The property tax levy campaign in 1989 demonstrated the level of division and disconnection within the organizational culture. The levy hadn't been updated in more than a decade. With the simple argument of increasing the levy to get the funding model to one-third from students, state, and local taxpayers, the college launched a levy campaign. Unfortunately, the controller at the college wrote an op-ed in the local newspaper to say that the taxpayers should not support the levy increase and the college had enough money already. The campaign could not recover from the negative press and the levy failed by 70 percent.

Despite the setback, the board continued its support for engaging the community in more meaningful ways and encouraged the new president to develop contacts and relationships throughout the community. Given the community response to the levy campaign, the timing seemed right to launch a new strategic planning process that engaged both the internal and external community.

With representatives from the board, faculty, staff, and administration, an Institutional Planning Council was formed. Several community-based focus groups and community conversations were held, along with extensive data collection and analysis from the University of Akron Research Institute. The result was "Vision 2000"—a strategic plan with seven strategic goals and no fewer than fifty initiatives.

This was a brand-new experience for the faculty, in particular, who were generally of the mind that they drove the curriculum and knew what the community needed. However, the process and information gleaned along the way seemed to turn the faculty more toward the needs of the external community. The college was also able to leverage the community-based planning process for important property tax levy campaigns as well. Over time, Vision 2000 completely changed the strategic orientation of the culture.

In 1997, LCCC formally pursued updating the strategic plan. By then the culture was ready to transition the Planning Council to a Vision Council that also included local community members. More than 150 community groups were engaged, in addition to several community summits that were convened to aggregate and analyze both quantitative and qualitative data. The process was guided by a revisiting and updating of the mission and core values and resulted in a new set of aggressive strategic goals and initiatives.

All college stakeholders were engaged in the process that connected with the entire governance process of the college's Faculty Senate and Staff Council. A key design element was pairing faculty and staff with community members during the community summits to personally hear what the community had to say. These interactions helped change attitudes and infused a new sense of openness and flexibility throughout the culture.

Getting Governance Right

LCCC was the only college in the region that was not unionized. A pair of faculty organizing efforts had failed (60 percent against) in 1986 and 1993. The first effort was in overall frustration with the somewhat absentee faculty leadership, but the second effort was more focused on involvement of the Board of Trustees in setting salary and benefits without presidential involvement.

This structure severely inhibited the process to address any nonfinancial concerns for faculty. Shortly after the second attempt to unionize failed, a mutual-gains process was put into place. Through a highly engaged process that was based on mutual agreements and involved data collection and analysis, as well as collaborative exploration of alternatives and joint agreement on success measures, the culture began to change. This work coincided with the implementation of the Vision 2000 Strategic Plan and really set the stage for the Vision Council in 1997.[21]

The Faculty Senate had existed, but a parallel Staff Council was created for the purpose of creating more transparent communication mechanisms. Additionally, the President's Cabinet was eliminated and replaced with an Operations Council that consisted of the president, vice presidents, and the leaders of the Faculty Senate, Staff Council, and Student Senate. Implementation teams and various groups provided weekly updates and presentations to the Operations Councils that required the leaders of the stakeholder groups to take those updates back to their respective peers.

Simultaneously, the administrative structure was altered based on the design principle that there should be no more than two layers of administration between the president and direct service to students and the community. The twenty-five administrators met monthly as the Administrative Leadership Team to address overarching issues and coordinate efforts. This required substantial delegation and new forms of leadership at all levels throughout the organization. All of these changes hardwired new behaviors and communication channels that contributed to increasing trust and empowerment that also helped shape the culture to become more adaptive and vibrant. [22]

Creating a Community of Learners

While the strategic planning process opened the eyes, hearts, and minds of a critical mass of faculty, staff, and administration to understand and embrace community needs, extensive professional development was critical to develop the skills necessary to address those needs in the most creative and efficient ways. No noticeable professional development infrastructure existed in 1987. Over time, structure was established and funding was provided to create a mechanism for supporting the ongoing development and enrichment of faculty and staff at the college.

Eventually, the research of the Gallup organization on employee engagement, Appreciative Inquiry resources at nearby Case Western Reserve University, and Kim Cameron's research from the Center for Positive Organizational Leadership at the University of Michigan were analyzed and applied to several initiatives. This ongoing commitment to relentlessly working on the culture so that people had regular opportunities to grow and learn made a difference. As Dr. Church shared, "As long as people are growing and learning, the institution inherently continues to grow and develop." [23]

One of the most powerful experiences developed from a need to communicate everything happening inside and outside the college. Quarterly brown-bag forums with faculty were created to further engage faculty in identifying trends and discussing issues through conversations built around data. Everyone's schedules were so full, these forums were structured in ninety-minute sessions over the lunch hour. Breakfast or lunch was provided in an informal setting to ensure that faculty could engage in meaningful dialogue around the data and trends.

After starting small, the forums slowly grew to eventually attract roughly half of the full-time faculty, further underscoring the level of interest, engagement, and commitment on the part of faculty in understanding trends and helping shape the college responses to those trends.

With enough acceptance and engagement in professional development, the culture was ready to position the college as an early adopter of the student completion agenda. LCCC become fully immersed in its completion transformation beginning in 2011 when it joined Achieving the Dream and was named as one of the three cohort institutions in Ohio of the Bill and Melinda Gates Foundation's Completion by Design.

As the stars aligned, Ohio also transitioned to become one of the nation's first of two states to move to 100 percent performance funding for completion. Together, these completion imperatives further focused LCCC's culture on student success and completion. LCCC's resulting success led to being named one of the ATD Leader Colleges within five years. Much of that success can be attributed to its culture and ability to incorporate strategic design thinking principles and strategies to design with the end in mind for student completion and success. These efforts created more safety and trust by depersonalizing the data and allowed people to more comfortably explore the meaning behind the data, as well as derive creative solutions from the insights gained in the analysis.

The ATD experience built on the college's earlier experience as a founding member of the Strategic Horizon Network that connected the College to other forward-thinking colleges focused on studying disruptive innovation and strategic thinking in industries outside of higher education. Similar to Northern Essex Community College, LCCC found SHN to be a tremendous catalyst that provided a consistent infusion of new ideas to prompt change within the culture.

Building on Momentum

From 1998 onward, changes became even more noticeable and things seemed to accelerate. As Dr. Church shared with me, "If people can see success, they begin to believe in the value of change and open up to even more change." This truth changed what is sometimes referred to as the "full-plate syndrome" or "initiative fatigue" where people feel they are working at their capacity and can simply not take on one more responsibility or engage in one more initiative.

With people fully engaged in change efforts and continually evolving programs and systems, things began to accelerate with the repeated success of new property tax levy campaigns. Repeating the Vision Council process to update the Vision 2000 Strategic Plan with the Vision 2010 Strategic Plan deeply reinforced and affirmed the institutional behaviors associated with such an inclusive and broadly engaged process. These same behaviors derived from community-based planning were applied to the all-important levy campaigns to increase local financial support of the college.

With the important lessons learned from the first levy campaign and the processes developed for planning, several changes were made to future campaigns. Rather than the formula approach to making the case, the college focused on added value, outcomes, and deliverables to the community. In addition, faculty and staff contributed $100,000 to the campaign to demonstrate their collective commitment prior to going to the community for a levy increase (as they would in all subsequent campaigns). Over the following twenty-five years, the college was able to successfully complete seven levy campaigns and quietly move the funding formula to roughly one-third student, state, and local support.

Transformation

From 1987 to 2016, this continuous attention to organizational culture yielded several artifacts that point to transformation. The community-based strategic planning process, repeated several times over the years, continued to strengthen the alignment between the needs of the community and the operation of the college.

In 1989, Lorain County had the highest percentage of adults with associate degrees, but the lowest percentage of adults with bachelor's degrees of any county in the state of Ohio. Consequently, the college established a University Partnership initiative and received local support through a successful property-tax levy. Ten years later, the County saw a 39 percent increase in adults holding a bachelor's degree and today, more than three thousand students are enrolled in more than forty bachelor's and master's degree programs delivered by thirteen university partners in the on-campus Roy A. Church University Center.

The processes developed for the strategic planning efforts led to the successful levy campaigns that provided the college with necessary resources. The external focus and openness to change developed through robust professional development helped connect the college to networks and other national initiatives that brought additional resources and inherently shaped programs and services that enhanced the college's focus on student and community success.

Exposure and familiarity with more complex funding streams and networks forced the college to become more comfortable with using data to drive change. An increasingly sophisticated use of data in planning and decision-making allowed for a more cohesive and integrated approach to organizational change.

Through all of the change, steadfast attention was paid to creating consistency and connection to an ongoing institutional narrative. The promises made to the community had to be realized when people interacted with the college and seen in the programs and services offered. The institutional narrative was equally critical inside the organization as well.

As the number of initiatives underway began to accelerate and expand, communication was essential to helping stakeholders put change into context and understand how they fit with a fast-moving organization that was doing anything but "coasting." The importance of understanding and telling the story of the organization became so centrally understood by the college that in 2016 they selected as their next president Dr. Marcia Ballinger, who had started her career at the college twenty-five years earlier as the Director of Marketing Outreach and Media Relations.

LESSONS LEARNED

The two most significant elements of transforming culture illustrated by these three cases are patience and leadership. Transforming culture takes time and requires steadfast attention, relentless effort, and leadership that is beyond stable, but also intuitive and strategic. The deep organizational change in each case was never about any one individual, department, or program; it was always about the greater whole of the organization.

When leading cultural transformation, emotions run high, obstacles appear from every angle, and competing priorities in the short term create distractions that require strength, positivity, courage, and resilience for the long-term success of the effort. All three of these case studies highlight lessons that include the importance of gaining trust, turning the college outward, creating a sense of urgency by establishing shared purpose through compelling goals, engaging others in pursuit of those goals, and overcoming challenges to achieve breakthrough and transformation.

Battle for Hearts and Minds

In each case, the new president made a priority to establish trust, credibility, and transparency in their leadership. This foundation of trust amplified the theme of how relationships are at the core of transforming culture. For example, in each case, the college had issues at the top as employees observed the dynamics of the senior leadership team. Whether it was an underperforming individual or team dysfunction, everybody quietly waited to see what the president would do.

All three scenarios included a president taking necessary actions by moving with surgical precision to make key personnel changes and send a message that difficult decisions can and will be made, and that the respect and dignity of individuals would be maintained. Transitions were made with little fanfare, which helped engender trust early on in the presidential tenure in each case and communicated how relationships, conflict, and underperformance would be handled.

Along the way, it was a battle for the hearts and minds of the faculty and staff—many of whom were wrestling with their internal nature to maintain the status quo and fight to keep things safe, secure and predictable. Several key cultural attributes were leveraged differently in each case. Employees were engaged, affirmed, and recognized to feel as important as students, or at least a close second.

Additionally, more assertive and positive employee behavior was encouraged to fundamentally alter the daily interactions throughout each organization. With the localized engagement of the new campuses at Central Piedmont, the new council structure at Lorain, and the appreciative inquiry at Northern Essex, in particular, trust was accelerated through changes in the way faculty and staff interacted and the way they felt about themselves, each other, the students, the organization, and the community.

Turn the Organization Outward

If society is ever-changing, so are the local communities served by community colleges. These three cases all highlighted the fact that the organizational culture of a community college needs to be outwardly facing with a widespread understanding that it must reflect the community it serves. If it turns too insular, the organizational culture risks making the entire college irrelevant.

It follows then that if a culture is focused on the needs of an ever-changing and external community to mirror those changes, the internal culture will always be evolving as well. All three of these presidents identified the need to reorient these community colleges toward their local communities to infuse new ideas and energy into the institution and strengthen the alignment with community needs.

In each case, external voices from the community were lifted up to inform the collective thinking and strategic processes. Meaningful external scans using quantitative and qualitative data infused new perspectives into each college that changed the conversations and provided opportunities for reflection among senior leaders, faculty, and staff.

Assumptions were challenged and opinions were complemented by greater access to common facts and important community indicators that exposed institutional shortcomings. The subsequent changes over time cultivated a more nimble, proactive culture in each case. As capacity for engaging the community grew, so did the ability to take on more change by integrating initiatives and developing a sense of momentum at each college.

Create a Sense of Urgency toward Compelling Goals

A common pattern for these transformation stories emerged in the way in which they began with presidents building on the importance of trust through initial relationships to create a platform for change with a new strategic plan. A comprehensive strategic planning process was used each time to create a sense of renewal and engage the culture in the future direction of the college.

Although the processes varied with regard to the use of consultants and the level of community involvement, all introduced new ways of operating and communicating within the culture. The planning process in each case helped reinforce new behaviors and strengthened the level of trust and credibility for the new president and their senior leadership teams.

An important qualification here is that these three cases happened to have this strategic planning element in common. Depending on the history or current status of strategic planning at a given institution, a different approach may be necessary. For example, a president may do a listening tour to identify five to seven major systems that need attention. To create a change agenda, design teams with college-wide representation can be established to benchmark best practices, infuse new ideas into the culture, and evaluate existing internal practices to create bold and daring recommendations for change. The result is a top-down (create design teams), bottom-up (recommendations that are supported and implemented) approach that may fit a particular culture at a particular time to create a sense of urgency and a platform for real change that builds momentum for more change in the future.

Engage Others in Continuous Learning and Improvement

The new initiatives in each case signaled things would be different and created internal discomfort within the culture. Employees were subsequently engaged through governance and supported through professional development to go about developing and implementing the initiatives in the new strategic plan. Employees were not only exposed to new information, experiences, and perspective, they also were given additional tools to keep expanding that exposure and application.

As new goals were established with new initiatives, the scope and pace of organizational life changed dramatically. This required new skills for faculty and staff as well as leadership at all levels in cultures that were more accustomed to mandates coming down from on high and using mandates or, at best, using the path of least resistance to get things done. It was critically important to find ways to continually introduce new ideas and energy into the institution and change the strategic orientation of each culture.

Exposure to outside networks along with extensive and ongoing professional development programs were key to cultural transformation in each case. And yet, when budgets are tight, why is it so common for colleges to pull back on travel and professional development as though they are nonessential "extras" in the annual budget? Similarly, each case intentionally kept employee recognition as a priority to fan the flames of innovation, reward risk, and amplify the fundamental behaviors that modeled the new culture.

Expect Struggle and Challenge

With a few exceptions, the struggles and challenges seemed more subtle and ongoing than flashpoints of significance. Each college had (and still has) varying degrees of tension between subcultures of employee groups (e.g., faculty and administration), departments and divisions, branch campuses and extension sites, and other aspects of internal pressure that create the distractions for any cultural transformation effort.

Granted, each president in these cases had their individual, significant moments, from lawsuits and unfortunate op-eds, to bold demonstrations of visible resistance. Other forms of struggle were evident through the discomfort created by engaging the external community in new ways and infusing outside voices. These perspectives opened the door to expand the amount of data shared throughout each college, which subsequently changed conversations and perspectives among faculty and staff.

The challenges illustrated in these cases underscore the importance of taking the long view and employing resilient, patient leadership. Challenge is normal and active resistance is to be expected, which is why culture change occurs over several years. In each instance, real forward movement took almost two years; traction with change, around four; tangibly different results in sustained behavior change, at five or six; palpable momentum, after seven or eight years; and transformation with ongoing evolution, after a decade or more.

Breakthrough and Turn the Flywheel

The steady, daily effort to transform organizational culture over several years in these three cases brings to mind the flywheel effect described by Jim Collins in his book *Good to Great.*

> Picture a huge, heavy flywheel—a massive metal disk mounted horizontally on an axle, about 30 feet in diameter, 2 feet thick, and weighing about 5,000 pounds. Now imagine that your task is to get the flywheel rotating on the axle as fast and long as possible. Pushing with great effort, you get the flywheel to inch forward, moving almost imperceptibly at first. You keep pushing and, after two or three hours of persistent effort, you get the flywheel to complete one entire turn.
>
> You keep pushing, and the flywheel begins to move a bit faster, and with continued great effort, you move it around a second rotation. You keep pushing in a consistent direction. Three turns . . . four . . . five . . . six . . . the flywheel builds up speed . . . seven . . . eight . . . you keep pushing . . . nine . . . ten . . . it builds momentum . . . eleven . . . twelve . . . moving faster with each turn . . . twenty . . . thirty . . . fifty . . . a hundred.
>
> Than at some point—breakthrough! The momentum of the thing kicks in your favor, hurling the flywheel forward, turn after turn . . . whoosh! . . . its

own heavy weight working for you. You're pushing no harder than during the first rotation, but the flywheel goes faster and faster. Each turn of the flywheel builds upon work done earlier, compounding your investment and effort. A thousand times faster, then ten thousand, then a hundred thousand.

The huge heavy disk flies forward, with almost unstoppable momentum. Now suppose someone came along and asked, "What was the one big push that caused this thing to go so fast?" You wouldn't be able to answer; it's just a nonsensical question. Was it the first push? The second? The fifth? The hundredth? No! It was all of them added together in an overall accumulation of effort applied in a consistent direction. Some pushes may have been bigger than others, but any single heave—no matter how large—reflects a small fraction of the entire cumulative effect upon the flywheel.[24]

It was striking during the interviews how the pace and tone in the voice of each of the three presidents changed after the story reached roughly year ten of their tenure. The tempo of their sentences increased. I could almost see the smiles through the phone. It was evident that as the metaphorical flywheel took hold in each of their respective institutions, the results were increasingly beyond anything they could have imagined when they first took the reins as president.

I remember calling Roy Church when I first became president at Mohawk Valley Community College. I was looking forward to seeing him at a conference and catching up on things. He said something like,

Randy, I'd love to connect, but I'm not going to be able to make it. I'm so darn busy here, I just can't get away right now. I can honestly say I'm busier now in my twentieth year than I was when I started. It's like when you just keep at it—over time, the momentum builds and the community and everyone around you just comes up with these great ideas that pull things together in such a way that you couldn't have possibly planned it all in advance!

Institutional Context

These three cases involved presidents whose tenure lasted twenty-nine, twenty-five, and fifteen years. Despite the different institutions located in three different regions (South, Northeast, and Midwest), with different funding and governance structures (one unionized, one not, and one nearly), with different enrollment and employee profiles and different organizational histories, they all shared common variables as previously described. However, they all started from a different place and leveraged opportunities unique to each college.

Initial Assessment

Central Piedmont had lost connection with its core value of innovation. By resurfacing the importance of that inspirational and aspirational value, the cultural change effort found traction and purpose. Lorain had turned insular and received a needed shock to the system by giving local community members a seat at the table in discussions about the college's future. With still a different starting point, Northern Essex needed to reduce the passive-aggressive behavior among employees who did not feel valued as they protected archaic processes and systems.

Unique Priorities

Growing out of the initial assessment, each college had to pursue cultural transformation from a different angle and use different levers. Central Piedmont leveraged the vision and process of expanding to a multicampus organization in a relatively short period of time. Lorain found leverage in overhauling the governance system and using the rhythm of bond-levy campaigns to engage employees and bring focus to the short- and long-term strategy of the organization.

Although Northern Essex activated the governance system for the strategic planning process, the big differentiator for cultural transformation was the focus on process management teams that inculcated the elements of continuous learning and improvement throughout the organization. Despite finding different levers, all three transformation efforts modeled new leadership, lifted up employees and supported new behaviors, clarified core values and organizational strategy and, over time, developed a more pervasive commitment to change.

CONCLUDING THOUGHTS

These three cases highlight the importance of culture in transforming community colleges. Despite several differences in organizational context and approaches, several common threads emerge in the analysis. Humble and driven leadership helped build trust that engaged employees in a shared purpose and strengthened a sense of community.

By increasing connections and trust, new perspectives were able to be shared and considered that helped create data-rich cultures engaged in continuous learning and improvement. This resulted in each institution becoming more outward facing, curious, and future focused to create a culture of anticipation as the external environment grew more complex. These important aspects of cultural transformation are the focus of the remaining chapters in this book.

NOTES

1. Cameron, K. S., and Quinn, R. E. (2011). *Diagnosing and Changing Organizational Culture: Based on the Competing Values Framework*. San Francisco: Jossey-Bass. 1.
2. Ibid.
3. Phelan, D. J. (2016). *Unrelenting Change, Innovation, and Risk: Forging the Next Generation of Community Colleges*. Lanham, MD: Rowman & Littlefield.
4. Baker, G. A. III. (1992). "Creative Cultures: Toward a New Paradigm." In *Cultural Leadership: Inside America's Community Colleges*, George A. Baker III and Associates (eds.), 1–16. Washington DC: Community College Press.
5. Collins, J. (2001). *Good to Great*. New York: HarperCollins, 1.
6. Ibid.
7. Hill, A. (2001). *Be Quick—But Don't Hurry: Finding Success in the Teachings of Lifetime*. New York: Simon & Schuster.
8. Interview with Dr. Tony Zeiss. November 23, 2016.
9. Ibid.
10. Ibid.
11. Interview with Dr. David Hartleb. January 7, 2017.
12. Ibid.
13. Ibid.
14. William Heineman. (2017). Personal communication. March 10, 2017.
15. Ibid.
16. *Interview with Dr. David Hartleb*, January 7, 2017.
17. Achieving the Dream. www.achievingthedream.org (accessed January 7, 2017).
18. Ibid.
19. Cooperrider, D., and Whitney, D. (2005). *Appreciative Inquiry: A Positive Revolution in Change*. San Francisco: Berrett-Koehler Publishers.
20. Interview with Dr. Roy Church. January 14, 2017.
21. Marcia Ballinger. (2017). Personal communication. May 26, 2017.
22. Ibid.
23. Interview with Dr. Roy Church. January 14, 2017.
24. Collins. (2001). *Good to Great*. 164–65.

Chapter Three

Driving Cultural Transformation through Leadership

Only three things happen naturally in organizations: friction, confusion, and underperformance. Everything else requires leadership.

—Peter Drucker

The leadership literature is vast and filled with frameworks, models, behaviors, and checklists. Applying these leadership tools to culture, however, is anything but a simple task. Boards of trustees, administrators, faculty, and staff share responsibility for building and maintaining a culture that is capable of embracing change and evolving the organization in response to changing demands. Although everyone contributes to culture simply by participating in it, leadership at all levels is necessary to shape culture by reinforcing positive norms and sustaining high performance.

The ubiquitous nature of culture makes changing it in any organization a complex phenomenon. Most community colleges have some aspect of the phrase "transforming lives" in their vision, mission, or values statements. We are all about changing lives, which makes it ironic that changing ourselves and our colleges should be so difficult. As humans, we tend to naturally gravitate toward what we believe to be familiar and safe.[1] And yet, in many instances, pursuit of the unfamiliar is actually the safest route for long-term survival of an organization. It is pursuit of the unfamiliar that requires leadership in all of its complexity.

When I was developing my dissertation topic years ago, I wanted to study the relationship between leadership style and organizational change. I was working for an amazing president in Colorado who had led our college through major change. When things got dark and were turning negative, her leadership and indelible spirit alone kept the organization moving forward. I wanted to understand more about the relationship between leadership and organizational change and use the dissertation process to study the phenomenon.

When reviewing my proposal, a committee member asked me if leadership was something that could truly be studied. She handed me an article by Alan Church[2] and asked, "After all, isn't leadership just a bundle of behaviors anyway?" I later learned she was discreetly and strategically pushing me to choose between leadership and change as my research focus in an attempt to narrow the scope of my study. That experience and the notion of "leadership as a bundle of behaviors" helped me choose organizational change as the focus of my dissertation and made the pursuit of the "right bundle of behaviors" in leadership a career-long quest.

CONTEXT FOR LEADERSHIP

Community colleges have never faced the complex array of change forces that surround them today. The external environment is increasingly harsh with some states like Arizona moving to abandon public support altogether for community colleges.[3] Elsewhere, state support reductions coupled with enrollment declines have made community college operating budgets increasingly dependent on student tuition increases that eventually compromise access. Performance funding has changed the game in states like Ohio, where 100 percent of state aid is based on performance.[4] The past ritual of simply ascending the capitol steps a few times a year to advocate for an increase in base aid is a fading reality across the country.

Beyond resources, today's community colleges are burdened with a dizzying array of legal shifts in financial aid regulations, Title IX requirements, and the Fair Labor Standards Act that require time, attention, and response.[5] Increased competition and disruptive technological changes create a level of dissonance and uncertainty never before experienced by institutions and leaders. Workforce demands from the private sector continue to increase in intensity, with employers calling for customized programs and graduates in technical programs that don't attract students in sufficient number to fill job openings.

With fewer resources and growing complexity, community colleges are embracing the student completion agenda that is bringing into question decades of perceived success, when in fact we just have not been measuring the right things. Community colleges are also faced with addressing the needs of increasingly diverse, underserved populations whose service needs outstrip available resources, as greater attention is needed for the "extracurricular" life needs of students—like transportation, childcare, food, and shelter. The support needs of students of color, veterans, refugees, immigrants, those in addiction recovery, the disabled, and those who fall in more than one of these categories test the resources and capacities of community colleges.

As change forces accelerate in intensity, many colleges find their internal cultures dominated by conversations about student preparation or mired in debates about small change in course schedules or the academic calendar. Leaders trying to overcome resistance to change—both overt and subtle—are surrounded by staff interested in tweaking, rather than redesigning, antiquated systems and processes designed for a time that has passed.

Skepticism with technological shifts like MOOCs (massive open online courses), open educational resources (OERs), and predictive analytics create distractions and clog communications while undermining the fundamental change these developments represent. In this new reality, many colleges are overwhelmed by contradictory forces of growing student and staff demands, diminishing resources, and intensifying calls for accountability. Lacking easy solutions, leaders find themselves in the company of a critical mass of faculty and staff experiencing burnout and fatigue.

LEADERSHIP PARADOX

In a context of fast change, simply managing change is no longer sufficient. Cultural transformation requires leadership capable of anticipating and responding to the condition of paradox. To guide and lead change, leaders must balance four emerging tensions that influence decision-making:

- Managing for today *or* tomorrow—The short-term needs of today may conflict with the long-term prospects for tomorrow. As Ford Motor Company CEO Jim Hackett said, "It is unrelentingly unfair that leaders must think about their organization in two frames simultaneously, the present and the future."[6] *Paradox*: leaders will need to simultaneously exercise patience and create a sense of urgency.
- Adhering to *or* crossing boundaries—Inertia is resident in the culture of every organization and can create boundaries that maintain the status quo. Leaders must consider the timing and the risk involved in crossing boundaries to promote organizational behaviors that guide cultures through change. *Paradox:* leaders will need to pursue opportunities for change outside the institution while simultaneously providing stabilizing touchstones for faculty and staff inside the institution.
- Maximizing value for the institution *or* generating wider benefits for community—As a taxpayer-funded enterprise, community colleges have an obligation to deliver benefit to communities above and beyond stated needs. Yet colleges have finite resources and the long-term future of the organization must be ensured. *Paradox:* leaders will need to find ways to

simultaneously balance value to the community with value to the college within the limits of available resources.

• Prioritizing students and staff *or* a broad audience of stakeholders—Who comes first: internal stakeholders or external community? There is no easy answer to this question and what is best depends on context and circumstance. On the one hand, who can downplay the importance of positioning a college to address big-ticket issues like economic development, poverty, literacy, early-childhood education, homelessness, and veterans' issues? On the other hand, however, these priorities can be perceived by some as a "distraction" from obvious institutional priorities like teaching and learning. *Paradox:* leaders will need to avoid "either-or" thinking about stakeholders and find ways to simultaneously value and serve the needs of multiple stakeholders inside and outside of the institution.

THE VALUE OF TIME

Cultural transformation takes time. Despite the obvious importance of these words, they are not very well understood by boards and a surprising number of presidents. In his forty-plus years at Tompkins Cortland Community College in New York with the last twenty-six as president, Carl Haynes found the culture there to shift in subtle but significant ways over many years.

> Bringing about a change in culture does not happen with any major initiative or grand plan; it's doing a lot of seemingly small things consistently over time that build trust in one's leadership. As trust builds for senior leaders, it gradually permeates the entire organization and increases approachability, transparency, and support for new ideas throughout the organization.[7]

My personal experience with change at Mohawk Valley over the last ten years reflects a similar pattern and duration for cultural transformation. My first two years were spent revealing the organizational culture through developing a new strategic plan and refining key systems and processes. MVCC's culture was visibly moving in a new direction within four years as new initiatives started to take hold. Transformation seemed to gain traction by year six and meaningful results and outcomes became manifest by year eight following implementation of a new strategic plan that built on early priorities. Finally, a full sense of momentum and clarity of new cultural norms was evident by the tenth year. Key aspects of leadership that connect with cultural transformation are important for institutions and leaders engaged in change, and are touched on in the remainder of this chapter.

Cultural Orientation

Leaders are more likely to be successful in driving change if they work with organizational culture over time, in contrast to pushing change overnight. As Carter and Alfred state, "Understanding culture helps leaders address deeply held, fundamental beliefs that could otherwise result in resistance. Acceptance of change is much more likely if arguments for it are framed in a manner that is consistent with the college culture and constructed in a way that respects past tradition."[8] Too often new presidents are asked or feel compelled to share their "vision" for the organization. Without a deep understanding of the culture and how it evolved, vision will not be meaningful and, if created prematurely, will not be shared by stakeholders.[9]

One way to help leaders understand culture is to start from the first day on the job or even earlier. When I interviewed for the presidency at Mohawk Valley, the SUNY chancellor at the time, Admiral John Ryan, asked me what I had done to prepare for the position. I responded with a summary of my experience and skills and he quickly put his hand up for me to stop. He then asked, "What have you done to prepare yourself to lead the culture of the college?" I did not have much of an answer. He told me to buy the book *You're in Charge—Now What?* upon my return to the airport to catch a flight home.[10]

That recommendation stands as one of the best pieces of advice I have ever received. I read this book that described how fifty Fortune 500 CEOs spent their first one hundred days on the job. The authors synthesized common themes from those experiences and provided advice for how new leaders should spend their first one hundred days. I modified their work to create what has become a cultural orientation process at Mohawk Valley.

I started with my assistant, who had been at the college for forty years, knew everyone, loved the college and community deeply, and approached her job like it was her hobby. I asked her a few simple questions:

1. How would you describe the culture of the college?
2. What needs to change?
3. What needs to be preserved?
4. What do people hope I do?
5. What do people hope I don't do?
6. Who are the three most respected people at the college?
7. Who are the next three people I should meet with to increase my understanding of the culture?

I then met with the three people she recommended and asked them the same set of questions and subsequently did the same with the people they recommended until I met with nearly fifty individuals. It was important for me to meet with people in their work space to send a message of openness, humility, and vulnerability. I took all my notes on the same notepad so that at the end of three weeks or so, I was ready to consolidate the full compendium of notes into a one-hundred-day plan. I worked with my board chair on refining the plan and used it as a communication tool with the rest of the board for the first three months on the job.

The experience was so useful that I had my new vice president for Learning and Academic Affairs follow the same process when she was hired a year later. Over the years, nearly all new administrators have followed the process to the point that even internal candidates have used it. When our Assistant Director of Admissions was promoted into the role of Director of Admissions, he requested the chance to complete the cultural orientation process even though he had worked at the college for eleven years. It helped him gain a better understanding of the college he would be promoting with a team on the road. He enjoyed the process so much that all new hires in admissions—recruiters and support staff—complete the process to better understand the culture they are representing to prospective students and families.

The process is organic as the random and emergent nature of the interviews leads to spontaneous interaction. Leaders new to the organization can quickly map informal power and influence networks by unobtrusively surfacing opinion leaders through informal inquiry. The process also quickly reveals a simple menu of early wins and opportunities for change in relationship to problems that have gone unnoticed or unaddressed over time as a consequence of internal dynamics and inertia.

Intentional informal inquiry such as this also has the advantage of sending positive messages to organizational units with new leaders and staff introducing themselves by traveling through halls and offices and experienced employees feeling affirmed by the experience of being suggested as someone who should be consulted to learn more about the makeup of culture. In recent years, this approach to cultural mapping was refined through Michael Watkins's work, *The First 90 Days*, and codified as our cultural orientation process.[11] (See appendix A.)

ALIGNED LEADERSHIP

Transforming culture is about weaving the cultural elements of an organization into a threaded and cohesive whole. Leading transformation efforts has much to do with creating the conditions for others to thrive, which is why the behavior of leaders is critically important as a facilitator or inhibitor of transformation. While flexibility is inherently important, consistency and alignment—staying on message and executing timely action over an extended period of time—are behavioral attributes that separate effective from ineffective leaders in cultural transformation. Real cultural transformation dies on every hill where a supervisor fails to model emotionally intelligent, thoughtful, and empowering leadership that communicates and reinforces an alignment with the core values and strategic direction of the college.

The Power of Connection

Trust is at the core of culture change and requires connection with leaders, no matter how large the organization. Whether leadership is located at the board level, the president's office, or other levels within the organization, cultural transformation is facilitated by thoughtful, disciplined, and emotionally intelligent action from those in a position to lead. While some situations may call for command-and-control leadership, the days of managing culture through mandates and directives are gone.

A more inclusive and mindful approach to leadership connecting leaders and staff through shared values and mutual bonds to the mission of the organization is essential in institutions pursuing transformation. Connectivity is not achieved through periodic effort—it must be nurtured day in and day out by leaders who understand the importance of consistency in behavior.

The modern workplace is full of leaders who give lip service to the importance of connectivity with employees, but do little about it. Organizations that do cross the bridge from thought to action in leader-employee alignment do so through decision-making strategies that put employees on equal footing with managers. Toyota employees, for example, can personally stop the production line in a manufacturing plant to address a quality or safety concern—an earmark of Toyota's culture of shared commitment and common purpose embedded in organizational processes and systems. [12]

The leadership philosophy at Whole Foods has been cultivated on principles focused on human connection. CEO John Mackey states, "We are now seeing a significant rise in the appreciation of 'feminine' values of caring, compassion, cooperation, and more right-brain qualities, heralding a harmonious blending of these human values in our work and life." [13]

Early in my career I was fortunate to be surrounded by mentors who exposed me to Kouzes and Posner's leadership research, and I have followed their work ever since. After studying survey results from more than 250,000 participants in 200 countries, Kouzes and Posner arrived at a simple but powerful model for leadership based on five core principles. [14]

1. Model the way.
2. Inspire a shared vision.
3. Challenge the process.
4. Enable others to act.
5. Encourage the heart.

Although the five principles were originally intended to outline characteristics of good leadership, they can be modified to create a model for leading change:

1. Build trust and respect (model the way).
2. Connect core values to a compelling future (inspire a shared vision).
3. Create a change agenda (challenge the process).
4. Engage others in pursuing the change agenda (enable others to act).
5. Celebrate successes and fan the flames of momentum (encourage the heart).

Modeling the way is the first leadership behavior for a reason—it is at the core of creating connections, establishing and nurturing relationships, and building trust. Goleman's work on emotional intelligence provides powerful applications of brain research to gain insights into the essence of human connection that form the basis of trust.[15] Leadership that models emotional intelligence helps to nurture positive and productive interactions within an organization by creating close, safe, and affirming relationships. Emotionally intelligent behavior increases the release of serotonin and dopamine in the central nervous system that contributes to feelings of well-being and happiness. These feelings have a positive influence on productivity and creativity that enhance individual and collective performance.

As David Katz, executive director of Organizational Development at Mohawk Valley, states,

> An emotionally intelligent leader cares about each member of the group; cares about the mutually beneficial and agreed upon goals of the group; cares enough to consider and encourage contributions and ideas from all; and helps folks see things in themselves that may be beyond their own self-belief. And most of all, gives others the tools and encouragement to reach those higher aspirations.[16]

Positive Leadership

A corollary to emotional intelligence is the research of Kim Cameron on positive organizational leadership at the Center for Positive Organizations in the Ross School of Business at the University of Michigan. Cameron's research aligns with Carol Dweick's work on the impact of mind-set on individual and organizational outcomes. A "growth mindset of abundance" treats failure as a learning opportunity. In contrast, a "fixed mindset of scarcity" views setbacks as the upper limit of possibility.[17]

Abundance is about doing more of what works well and believing in an ever-expanding set of possibilities and resources. Scarcity emphasizes what needs to be fixed in the current context and redistribution of limited resources. Positive leadership is influenced by elements associated with abundance. "It emphasizes an affirmative bias, or a focus on strengths and capabilities and affirming human potential. . . . Without being Pollyannish, it stresses positive communication, optimism, and strengths, as well as the value and opportunity embedded in problems and weaknesses.[18] Cameron defines the essence of positive leadership as the following:

> Positive leadership emphasizes what elevates individuals and organizations (in addition to what challenges them), what goes right in organizations (in addition to what goes wrong), what is life-giving (in addition to what is problematic or life-depleting), what is experienced as good (in addition to what is objectionable), what is extraordinary (in addition to what is merely effective), and what is inspiring (in addition to what is difficult or arduous). It promotes outcomes such as thriving at work, interpersonal flourishing, virtuous behaviors, positive emotions, and energizing networks.[19]

At first, positive leadership comes across as simplistic and surface-level rhetoric: "just be positive!" It is much more and it is a cornerstone of leadership in cultural transformation. Positive leadership requires focus and intentionality on the part of leaders and it is the basis upon which leader-follower trust, organizational momentum and, ultimately, cultural transformation are built. The modern workplace is not inherently satisfying. Frustration abounds as a result of uneven distribution of work, miscommunication and lack of transparency, pressure for performance, unrealistic or unknown expectations, and a host of other variables that shape work experience.

Leaders are capable of fostering positive work environments that nurture a buoyant organizational culture. Cameron identifies three fundamentals for a positive workplace: compassion, forgiveness, and gratitude.[20] Compassion is a critical feature of organizations in which leaders encourage a culture of connection, sharing, and noticing that motivates staff to pay attention to what is happening with colleagues around them. Forgiveness is the key to resilience in a positive culture. In troubled times, leaders take action to provide visible support and model behavior that reinforces higher purpose in an organization.

The importance of language expressing forgiveness cannot be overstated, and it is the role and responsibility of leaders to help guide vocabulary in the organizational narrative when forgiveness is necessary. Gratitude is the final component of an organizational culture wired with positivity. Finding ways, big and small, to allow expressions of gratitude to permeate the organization is an important responsibility of leadership.[21] Whether creating handwritten notes of thanks or encouragement, informal "who made your day?" processes, or formal recognition programs, enabling expressions of gratitude by providing accessible systems will make gratitude a self-perpetuating feature of a positive organizational culture.

In organizations where compassion, forgiveness, and gratitude are resident, positive energy networks are more likely to develop if a leader is aware of their power. In *How Full is Your Bucket?*, Gallup authors Rath and Clifton provide a simple but powerful metaphor of a bucket.[22] They declare that we begin each day with a bucket full of energy and encounter people throughout the day that either add to the energy bucket or drain the bucket. To positively influence organizational culture, leaders must be "bucket fillers" and add to everyone's bucket through as many opportunities as possible.

Empirical research has shown that people who are considered positive energizers increase positive feelings and motivations in others and subsequently add to positive energy in the organization through a layered set of increasingly positive interactions and experiences.[23]

"Being a positive energizer makes individuals four times more likely to succeed than being at the center of an information or influence network."[24] A cascading effect takes hold in the organization as positivity grows in staff through interaction with positive energizers.[25] Armed with this information, savvy leaders find ways to develop networks of positive energy throughout the organization. They invest time and energy in identifying and supporting positive energizers and positioning them in ways to maximize their effect on colleagues and the organization as a whole. Simultaneously, they use energy networks to identify and address negative energizers.

For every aspect of an energy network influenced by positive energizers, the exact opposite holds true for negative energizers. Cameron provides a simple four-step approach to deal with a negative energizer. Provide honest and direct feedback; provide development opportunities to change behavior; isolate the individual to minimize their negative effect on others; and if all else fails, help the individual transition to a place outside the organization where they can succeed.[26]

Boards of Trustees

Governing boards have significant influence on organizational culture in community colleges. Their most important responsibility is to hire, orient, guide, challenge, support, and evaluate the president.[27] Unfortunately, many boards find themselves replacing presidents at a pace far swifter than they would like. The average tenure of presidents in community colleges is less than six years.[28] In the span of three academic years, from fall 2013 to spring 2016, more than 730 of the nation's 1,132 community college presidents (64 percent) turned over.[29]

Cultural transformation takes time, often a decade or more. With regular turnover in presidencies, meaningful cultural change is unlikely at many, perhaps most, community colleges in the nation. Like the archetype of faculty and staff standing in the hall watching leaders come and go, revolving leadership can hardwire a cultural belief that "this too shall pass" and create significant resistance to well-intentioned cultural transformation efforts.

Although presidential turnover can be attributed to special circumstances or personalities, a growing number of separations result from an ever-shrinking pool of qualified candidates[30] and the inability of boards to find the right leader for the institution at that time and place, or to create a positive environment that allows a president, and a college, to thrive. Boards must recognize the significance of their role in shaping culture and serving as a stabilizing force in organizational change.

Unfortunately, however, all too often board dynamics become a major distraction for a college. I have witnessed board members lock into a 6–5 or 4–3 voting pattern for years at a time, with votes based on political interests in contrast to the best interest of the institution. Board members dabbling in personnel decisions, meeting directly with staff on college issues, or involving themselves in purchasing contracts with vendors can create dissonance and uncertainty for staff.

Some boards record their board meetings for public access television or the Internet in an effort to increase transparency for the public. While most intentions may be good, some board members use the telecasts as an opportunity to grandstand and sidetrack board discussion. If not managed effectively, broadcasting dysfunctional behavior for all to see can bring negative media coverage to colleges whose mission is to serve students and the community and not the ego needs of board members.

The high-water mark for me in board dysfunction was to watch the majority voting bloc on a perpetually divided board silence the voice of a board member in the minority by using Robert's Rules of Order. While the vote was occurring, lights went on in the back of the boardroom and everyone turned around to see what was happening. The isolated board member had anticipated he would be silenced and had quietly excused himself to the back of the room, where he had invited local news media to hold a press conference to state his opinion and frustration with his board colleagues. The topic of discussion is lost on me, but it undoubtedly had little to do with student success or policy that might guide productive organizational change.

In contrast, boards exercising a hands-off approach to stewardship can end up serving as a rubber stamp for administration. If a college is effectively managed, this dynamic can work fine, but at a price of leaving a board out of touch with leaders and staff, college culture, and connection to the community. Disengaged boards can accelerate presidential transitions through neglect of issues that could be resolved by challenging presidents at the right time and right place. Board culture and behavior can affect organizational change as a function of its capacity to find a productive level of engagement with college and community.

Change is a deliberative process that is helped or hindered by the mindset and capabilities of a board. Recognizing the centrality of boards to college performance, the Association of Community College Trustees (ACCT) offers nine essential principles for effective board performance:

1. Act as a unit.
2. Represent the common good.
3. Set policy direction for the college.
4. Employ, support, and evaluate the college's chief executive.
5. Define policy standards for college operations.
6. Monitor institutional performance.
7. Create a positive college climate.
8. Support and advocate the interests of the institution.
9. Lead as a thoughtful, informed team.[31]

These principles may pose challenges to some colleges given the outlook and behavior of individual board members. At the core of creating a healthy board subculture is attention paid to developing relationships among board members. Trust among peers is a necessary foundation for managing conflict productively. Boards that are able to introduce diverse ideas, share dissimilar perspectives, disagree in respectful ways, and reach consensus on meaningful solutions provide a necessary foundation for initiating and managing change.[32]

Presidents and Senior Leaders

The extent to which presidents influence and lead cultural transformation is variable depending on their view of organizational culture. I have met presidents who feel they cannot be held responsible for the morale of their employees. Presidents holding this view believe morale is a matter of individual disposition and is not subject to change. In short, they believe leaders are incapable of impacting individual disposition. Leaders of this stripe do not take responsibility for organizational culture. Culture is a fixed element of the organization beyond the control of leaders. Accordingly, leaders should focus their attention on things they can control, like budget, fund-raising, strategic planning, and partnerships.[33]

In sharp contrast, a growing number of presidents view culture as a critical priority, and in some cases a top priority. As Eric Murray says in his role as president of Cascadia College near Seattle:

> My desire to be a president came only after watching other presidents fail to create a positive climate where their employees could thrive and do their very best to assist students. I steward the institution, which includes creating a culture our employees embrace and helping them be their very best. Making

the campus a place where employees want to spend their time, feel valued, and can share their enthusiasm for the learning process with our students is paramount to my role. And in turn, it helps students succeed because they feel the investment and support from our faculty and staff. This is simply a part of the mission.[34]

This is where trust and transparency come into play. Presidents and senior leaders are watched closely by staff throughout the organization. An insight that has stayed with me throughout my career came from a president who responded, when asked how she kept such an upbeat demeanor at all times, "Well, Randy, you can never forget that everyone notices when the boss isn't smiling. If I'm not smiling, people might wonder if they should have reason not to smile themselves!"

A vibrant organizational culture needs a vibrant leader—someone who understands that people need leaders to bring positive energy, resilience, and humility to work every day. As the number one cheerleader and chief storyteller for the organization, the president must bring his or her best every day. Anything less can derail workplace culture faster than one might think.

Beyond personal behavior and leadership style, a significant influence of presidents on organizational culture is the administrative structure they establish and how they staff it. The structure and dynamics of the senior leadership team can take a variety of forms ranging from managing relationships among members to toiling endlessly to develop a strategic focus. The extent to which presidents are successful depends on the effort they put forth and the dynamics they create. If presidents opt to meet with leadership team members individually, in contrast to collectively, the likelihood of creating a functional team dynamic is minimal.

Perhaps the greatest challenge in leadership is building a high-performing team. This takes time and effort, but has the potential to influence culture in positive ways. Patrick Lencioni's framework for high-performing teams (see figure 3.1) includes five elements that must be in place for teams to be effective. The absence of any one of these elements can create dysfunction within a team.[35]

As in personal relationships, trusting others and making oneself vulnerable do not come easily for many people, and yet, they are the foundation of high-performing team dynamics. Managing productive conflict is a skill not as commonly found among leadership teams as one might think. Conflict management requires intentional effort to build a pool of shared meaning through crucial dialogue culminating in appreciation and understanding of multiple perspectives, mutual respect, and joint commitment toward common goals.[36]

Leaders at All Levels

An engaged board, a visionary president, and a functional senior leadership team may not be enough to transition a culture to higher ground. A culture will remain resistant to change if leaders are not aligned in the pursuit of change at all levels in the organization. Alignment requires attention to the hiring process, employee engagement and support, empowerment, and consistent communication over time.

The extent to which administrative, faculty, and staff leaders employ consistent behavior in the pursuit of change is a key factor in cultural transformation. When leadership behavior is consistent across departments and divisions, alignment can be observed, thereby increasing morale and productivity while minimizing distractions and negativity. Alignment requires leaders at every level to model and reinforce behaviors of connection, affirmation, and accountability.

Unfortunately, senior leaders all too frequently think they are the primary difference makers in culture, and overlook the effect of mid-level supervisors in direct contact with staff. Tailored employee orientation programs can go a long way toward instilling a positive cultural outlook in newly hired faculty and staff. But if new employees go to work with direct supervisors who are distant, commanding, and condescending, they can quickly become part of the figurative "CAVE Society" (Colleagues against Virtually Everything) that rallies resistance to organizational change.

Senior leaders must be cognizant of connecting change efforts to leaders at all levels in the organization through blended and cohesive messaging

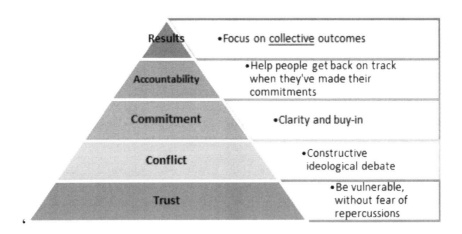

Figure 3.1.   High-Performing Team Framework. Lencioni, P. (2002). *Five Dysfunctions of a Team: A Leadership Fable.*

based on common experience. Common experience reinforces behavior that binds divisional and departmental subcultures to a common fabric that is part and parcel of the larger organizational culture. This is advanced through a cohesive administrative structure anchored in forward-thinking leadership behaviors. When this framework is nurtured and allowed to flourish over time, everyone wins—the organization as a whole, students, faculty and staff, and the community.

LEADING CHANGE

Change is a complex phenomenon that requires strategy and constant monitoring. Whether it be the scale of change—large or small—or the pace at which change is to occur, leaders must consider their role in managing the process. When combined with strategy, factors of scale and pace can provide leaders with necessary levers to transform organizational culture.

Determining the Scale of Change

Leading change requires a general sense of the scale and rhythm of change as well as factors that influence perceptions of change. Borrowing from the biological sciences, Tushman and Romanelli use the punctuated equilibrium model to describe phases in the life of organizations. Their research describes organizations as living organisms that experience change as all species do— through a series of punctuated changes separated by periods of equilibrium and stability. [37]

While change in species may take thousands, or even millions, of years, organizations experience change in a matter of years and, in some cases, months. Managing the length, frequency, and intensity of punctuations as well as periods of equilibrium requires intentioned leadership.

Unfortunately, all too many leaders have only a cursory understanding of change and the ripple effect their decisions have on organizational culture. Earlier in my career I served as a senior administrator in a college with a twenty-year system president who intentionally managed change and developed a single college culture in a multicampus district. After a brief period with an interim president, the Board of Governors hired a president whose previous experience was limited to single-campus colleges with enrollment a fraction of the size of the district I worked in.

In the first month on the job, the new president reorganized the administration into decentralized campus deans and, in so doing, fractured the single-college culture. Over the next eighteen months, the culture was battered by nonstop change. Academic affairs was charged with the task of reorganization. As the hiring for new positions began, the president changed the structure again on short notice—the president "re-orged the re-org" in real time.

Seven different marketing directors were hired and fired in just seven months. An existing employee was appointed as the new Director of Public Safety and then "unhired" and returned to his former position the following day. A course scheduling process that had been developed over several years with measurable success was changed overnight on the basis of an ill-informed presidential edict.

Careless alterations of this type throw cultures into shock and set an organization on its heels. The core values, norms, and beliefs that carry an organization through highs and lows are compromised and core relationships holding a culture together are placed in jeopardy. After two years, the president transitioned elsewhere and the executive vice president was hired as interim to stabilize the organization and heal the culture. He was eventually hired as the permanent president, and continues to build on culture as a lever for transformation in a once-again thriving and high-performing institution.

Examples of cultural resilience abound in community colleges. One of the better examples I encountered was part of the experience of chairing an evaluation team for an accreditation visit. The team and I found more than the average story during our visit. A few years earlier, the Board of Governors had hired a president who experienced trouble early in his tenure. It took the board a year to determine that a change was necessary and another year to navigate a presidential transition.

After a year with an interim president, more time was needed to complete an extended search process. At one point during the interim period the entire nine-member senior-leadership team was interim. And yet, key initiatives continued, strategic and departmental plans were executed, retention rates and enrollment increased, and new programs were developed. In the words of a staff member, "The culture here is strong. During the interim period the joke in the hallway was that if this organization was a living thing, it was dead from the neck up."

With a new permanent president in place who understood and leveraged culture, the college had a very successful accreditation outcome despite the rocky transitions. Strong, healthy, and resilient cultures can endure significant threats and challenges and remain vibrant over time for the benefit of students and the community.

While some cultures are subjected to the shock of continuing change, other cultures drag through periods of extended equilibrium. This is perhaps most evident when presidents stay too long and retire on the job, distance themselves from the organization, or simply stop driving and supporting change. Culture begins to fray around the edges and faculty and staff retreat to the bare minimum. The organization begins to drift and breaks down into insular units that stop communicating with one another.

The old saw "too much of anything may not be good" has a distinctive application to culture. Achieving a healthy balance between periods of punctuated change and productive equilibrium is critical if leaders are to bring faculty and staff on the journey of cultural transformation.

Determining the Pace of Change

Beyond tending to the scale of change, finding the right rhythm and pace for change in an organization requires close attention to culture. What are the opinion leaders thinking? How is the organization performing on key metrics? What initiatives are underway and at what capacity levels? What is the organization's recent history with initiatives: how many have been successfully implemented, how many have failed, how many are pending? To what extent is initiative fatigue apparent? These are the types of questions leaders must ask themselves to monitor organizational capacity for change. Additionally, change requires careful attention to relationships that must be developed and nurtured through culture.

In theory, organizational change should follow an orderly course and proceed at a pace within cultural boundaries. Five steps are fundamental:

1. Understand the basics: learn the culture and align the mission, vision, and values.
2. Forge strategy: clearly state the problem for stakeholders, engage them in developing shared solutions, and create an action plan.
3. Identify champions: connect stakeholders to the process in meaningful ways and identify change champions to lead the effort.
4. Support innovation: encourage alternative processes, encourage risk-taking behavior, and pay attention to the capacity of the organization to implement and sustain innovation.
5. Communicate and celebrate success: pay attention to messaging and regular communication and find ways to celebrate that foster the most important elements of the culture.[38]

In reality, however, organizational change is often a nonlinear process full of unknowns and unpredictable setbacks. Mandates will not dictate process and are likely to inhibit change beyond the initial directive. This is why effort must be made to involve stakeholders in the process, paying close attention to their level of understanding and engagement in change. Essential to engagement is opening staff to the idea that problems are opportunities for learning and growth, both individually and organizationally. Creating stronger connections with the external environment increases the level of information and stimuli coming into the organization. In Michael Fullan's words,

> Learning organizations know that expectations and tensions in the environment contain the seeds of future development. There are far more ideas "out

there" than "in here." Successful organizations have many antennae to tap into and to contribute to the demands of change which are constantly churning in the environment. They treat the internal and external milieu with equal respect.[39]

Understanding employee mind-sets on change requires ongoing attention. It goes without saying that a positive correlation exists between how people perceive change and the extent to which they place change in a larger context and become involved in it as well.[40] This requires connectivity to the big picture and connecting micro and macro changes in an ongoing change narrative. Once a change narrative is established, what was formerly exceptional becomes routine and staff feel a sense of ownership over change that is underway. Change becomes ingrained in culture and routinized through repeated practice. Organizational change is like a muscle in the human body—the more you exercise it, the stronger and more familiar it grows.

Resourcing Change through Abundance

Driving change requires resources, and the manner in which leaders allocate resources can have a profound impact on organizational culture. Leaders send clear signals about priorities through resource decisions. In an environment of rising costs and diminishing resources, budgetary challenges grow increasingly significant. Resource challenges are conflated with communications that are hampered by the complexity of revenue streams like operating, capital, donations, and grants. Most employees are not close enough to budget development to understand seemingly mixed messages that arise.

For example, when vacancies are not being filled and employees are being laid off while additional staff are hired on a new grant, the cognitive dissonance among some employees creates rancor in the hallways. Similarly, when new equipment is not purchased or reductions are made to operating budgets while a new building is constructed, leaders must redouble their efforts to explain the difference between capital and operational funding streams to keep morale from slipping through misunderstandings among faculty and staff about revenue streams.

Against these and other challenges, how are leaders to drive change with fewer resources and employees stretched to capacity? Some presidents respond with a focus on "weathering the storm" versus driving change with across-the-board cuts—for example, a 3 percent reduction to every cost center. Others may employ hiring and salary freezes or scale back travel and professional development.

Imagine a president focused on being "more transparent and honest" who opens the new academic year at an all-college meeting with remarks emphasizing how bad the financial picture looks; enrollment, retention, and graduation rates are disappointingly low; and highlighting that it's uncertain how long this dark period will last so everyone will just have to work harder until the college hopefully gets through it.

There is a time and place for transparency, but opening the new academic year should be infused with messages of optimism and inspiration, underscoring the importance of abundance, particularly in the face of difficult challenges.

Beyond the uninspiring messaging, some of these strategies may work to balance an annual budget, but they can impact the culture of an organization years into the future. They contribute to a growing organizational mind-set of scarcity: resources are scarce so decisions are keyed to survival and maintenance. Organizations that do not grow and develop are at risk of stagnation and ultimately failure.

An alternative approach to resourcing and driving change through these challenges is to nurture an organizational mind-set of growth and abundance—an approach centered on what is working well and a belief that the necessary resources can be acquired through collaboration, creativity, and focused effort. Alfred, Shultz, Jaquette, and Strickland define a college of abundance through characteristics across twelve variables.

1. Managerial emphasis—building upon strengths and valuing assets
2. Cohesion—leaders and staff work in teams bound by common purpose
3. Resources—exceptional resources through leveraging
4. Resource perspective—primary emphasis on intangible resources
5. Organizational architecture—holistic; organization emphasizing unity
6. Operational focus—process and system innovation
7. Risk—embrace and reward risk and change
8. Collaboration—college is the hub of an expansive network
9. Competitive focus—collaborating with rivals for mutual gain
10. Performance objective—stretch and leveraging
11. Leadership—leaders throughout the organization
12. Attractiveness—capable of attracting quality staff throughout the institution[41]

Resourcing change through abundance is possible by finding ways to leverage all available resources and pursuing organizational stretch at every opportunity. By going beyond the tangible elements of financial, physical, human, and technological resources, colleges can identify new possibilities and considerations. Intangible resources like systems, policies, processes, as well as leveraging institutional reputation, networks, and partnerships to identify new capacity and collaborations can surface solutions that would otherwise be invisible behind a cloud of scarcity and myopic thinking. Abundance also calls for a strengths-based approach that looks to maximize leadership at all levels and make the most out of all available assets.

The authors go on to say that abundance is

> more than a matter of people and commitment because if staff do not have the resources they need to operate, abundance will be difficult to achieve. Finally, while a talented president and effective leaders figure prominently into abundance, they cannot, in and of themselves, guarantee its achievement. As an organizational state, abundance is a product of many factors coming together at the same time to leverage performance.[42]

For the past several years in most states across the country, the continued decline in funding from state and local sources feels like a continuous wave of unrelenting negativity that inculcates an oppressive feeling of despair and scarcity on many college campuses. In contrast to the president described above, picture a college president facing similar budget, enrollment, and other dismal realities needing to provide opening remarks at the all-college meeting to start the year—only with an approach of abundance.

The message is focused on the important role the college plays in the community; the inspiring work everyone does on behalf of the students; a quick review of some of the challenges followed by a personal belief that the college is resilient and always has been; and the more everyone can work together and support each other in these difficult times, the faster the college can pull through this challenging period and emerge stronger than ever. The likelihood of faculty and staff approaching their jobs with an uplifted spirit is far more likely when hearing messages of abundance than the misplaced transparency resident in messages of scarcity.

Leaders can influence the overall institutional response to challenges like resource constraints by setting a tone that reinforces the characteristics of abundance and recasting obstacles as opportunities that can inspire collective action to rise to the occasion. An abundance-oriented organization will find ways to consistently reinforce hope over despair and identify new resources, leverage existing resources, and position itself for the future through new ways of thinking and operating.[43]

An abundance approach to resourcing change can be effective in navigating the difficult process of cultural transformation. How can faculty and staff focus on creativity and innovation when their coworkers are laid off, their workload increases, and new initiatives are announced on a regular basis? Resources must be reallocated to feed the parts of the organization that need to grow while simultaneously managing the elimination of programs and other reductions in the areas that are no longer viable or need to be realigned to operate differently in a different future context.

The principles of abundance previously described can be used to lead an organization through challenging times by leveraging resources and optimizing creativity that leads to innovation. Colleges of abundance are able to embrace the paradoxical notion of addition by subtraction. Despite seemingly fewer traditional resources, core elements of the culture and organization are preserved, the collective focus and strategy remains on the future, efficiencies are identified, and new initiatives are launched. Despite every excuse for decline and underperformance, a virtuous cycle of growth, innovation, and increased success continues.

LEADING FOR EQUITY AND INCLUSION

Over the past three hundred years, postsecondary institutions in America were designed for white males, ages eighteen to twenty, with time and money to spare. This profile only represents about a third of the current undergraduate population because in the past fifty years, the elements of college campuses have changed. More specifically, the students and the issues have grown dramatically different, particularly on community college campuses.

Today, 38 percent of all undergraduates are older than twenty-five; 58 percent work while enrolled in college; enrollment among Hispanic students has tripled and Black student enrollment has grown by 72 percent in the past twenty years; almost half of today's students are on their own financially; out of 4.8 million postsecondary students who are parents, 61 percent of those have no money to contribute to the cost of college.[44] Additionally, research from the Hope Lab at the University of Wisconsin, in a study of 33,000 students at seventy community colleges in twenty-four states, found that more than 50 percent of students are food insecure and 14 percent are homeless.[45]

Today's undergraduate student profile is dramatically different than the stereotypical characteristics so many Americans carry with them as the default college student archetype. And although many community colleges have indeed made changes—like offering special TRIO programs, wraparound support services, gender-neutral bathrooms, campus food pantries, and the like—the basic assumptions, systems, structures, and overall campus environment today remains a space where white males with time and money to spare are most comfortable and everyone else must work to find their space. Changing campus culture for equity and inclusion requires leadership.

DeRionne Pollard, president of Montgomery College, shares:

> Higher education was a moment before it was a series of buildings to be managed. To that end, one of the compelling issues for community college leadership now and into the future will be emphasizing our commitment to our social justice mission of access while also responding to increased calls for mission contraction and efforts to limit higher education participation.[46]

Beyond the social justice argument of infusing equity and inclusion into the culture of an organization because it is the right thing to do to level the playing field for all students, the idea of innovation should be the first element in case making for change. Most every college recognizes the need to innovate in the current environment.

As Morgan Stanley Vice Chairwoman Carla Harris says:

> Innovation is about ideas and ideas are about perspective. The more perspectives you have, the greater the range of ideas you have. Perspectives come from experiences so the more experiences you have, the more ideas you have. The more ideas you have, the more innovation will be present within your organization. That is why diversifying your workforce and making equity and inclusion a signature part of your culture will help you increase innovation. [47]

Despite this link between innovation, equity, and inclusion, culture remains a primary barrier to organizational change. Community colleges continue to pride themselves on serving this country as the primary access point to postsecondary education for our society's disenfranchised and underrepresented citizens. Unfortunately, countless attempts to fill vacancies with diverse candidates have been thwarted by nuanced and veiled words and actions on ineffective screening committees that marginalize and sideline qualified, potential, diverse candidates.

This reality continues to limit the number of role models on staff for students to look up to and connect with, which contributes to limits in strategies to accelerate student success efforts. As Marcia Ballinger, president of Lorain County Community College, says: "Leading community colleges to create equity-focused results that eliminate achievement gaps among our underrepresented groups of students so that they can improve economic mobility means that we must look internally to be intentional about our culture, policies, and practices."[48]

So how might leaders approach something as overwhelming as changing culture to increase diversity, equity, and inclusion? Damon Williams offers a useful framework for understanding what he calls the dimensions of dynamic diversity DNA.[49]

Williams states that the framework "is not a commentary on an organization's culture or its movement from being a space of exclusion to one of inclusion, although it stands to reason that if an institution is moving more intentionally and allocating resources, the institutional culture should become more diverse and inclusive in response to those efforts."[50] However, from a practitioner's perspective, the framework has great application and provides useful guidance for identifying the critical components of what it takes to change culture in this realm.

To step forward and lead for equity and inclusion, leaders must pay close attention to the nuanced language and behavior around these issues as they

Table 3.1.   Dimensions of Dynamic Diversity DNA

Strategic Diversity Idea	The way diversity is defined and how the institution engages diversity as a matter of strategic priority
Diversity Infrastructure	Presence of dedicated institutional diversity offices, initiatives, and committees, particularly at senior levels of leadership and governance
Senior Leadership Support	Presidential and provost level support that includes the commitment of academic deans, senior administrative leaders, and faculty governance systems
Strategic Planning Systems	Presence of logistical and staff resources to guide the campus community in an inclusive stakeholder process that produces a strategic diversity plan
Change Activation Techniques	Presence of incentive, accountability, and reporting systems to drive, reward, and encourage change, along with effective systems for assessing and, when necessary, revising the plan and redirecting resources and activities
Resources	Presence of staff, financial, and other resources to implement strategic diversity plan

Williams, D. (2013). *Strategic Diversity Leadership*, 194.

appear in the culture. Communications, policies, norms, hiring processes, and other aspects of the culture can harbor subtle bias to maintain the status quo and preserve the uneven scales of success against students of color and other disenfranchised groups.

Equity and inclusion efforts require leveraging every bit of trust and credibility to frame the issues and create space for crucial conversations, as described earlier. Finding champions for the cause, like any other change, is critical to engage colleagues and move toward a critical mass within the culture to identify what and how things need to change. Perhaps the most obvious but yet overlooked strategy is to engage employees and, perhaps even more importantly, students in telling their stories to surface the array of challenges and unintended barriers institutions create for populations other than young, white males.

TRANSFORMING CULTURE

The ultimate measure of a leader's impact on culture is the performance of an organization, division, department, or team after the leader is gone. Too often, seemingly successful organizations have difficulty navigating transitions when boards have been lulled into complacency, employees have retreated into subcultures, or problems that were made to go away continue to manifest themselves.

Cultures implode when leaders put their personal interests at the forefront of decisions. If decision-making is designed to maintain stability and avoid change, the momentum that colleges need to navigate a dynamic environment can be squandered and result in unintended consequences. Strategic components that impact performance—labor contracts, finances, and enrollment management—can come apart and send leaders and staff into rescue mode and, worse yet, shifting time and energy away from opportunity.

Accrediting bodies and state auditors surface situations of this type all too frequently in the form of leaders who put their organizations at risk when they build structures, programs, and partnerships that they alone champion, and staff simply execute on behalf of the boss. These innovations may appear to be pioneering in the short term, but can fade away or fall apart once the leader is gone.

Organizational performance can be enhanced in the short term through a variety of strategies, but a healthy culture with staying power is characterized by leaders and staff guided by core values and a shared vision as they collectively pursue continuous improvement. In *Built to Last*, Collins and Porras provide a meaningful metaphor for leadership that is needed to foster a durable healthy culture.[51]

Leaders who operate with all of the answers and all decisions flowing through them are focused on keeping the official time and telling others what time of day it is. The problem with this approach is that when that leader is gone, no one knows what time it is and the culture is adrift in confusion. In contrast, leaders who place priority on the long-term success of the organization focus their energy on "clock building" to provide mechanisms for the time to be known throughout the culture regardless of who is sitting in the corner office.

Clock building within a culture requires commitment to building and refining systems that are self-correcting and continuously improving. These systems are possible in cultures that are data infused and capable of using data to optimize operations. Mechanisms for environmental scanning, forecasting, and strategic thinking are fully developed in these cultures as a means for anticipating change and disruption. These requisites of healthy cultures—meaningful employee engagement, data-informed decision-making, and strategic thinking—are topics that will be pursued in the closing chapters of the book.

NOTES

1. Pettigrew, A. M. (1985). "Examining Change in the Long-Term Context of Culture and Politics." In *Organizational Strategy and Change*, J. M. Pennings, and Associates (eds.), 269–318. San Francisco: Jossey-Bass.
2. Church, A. H. (1995). "Linking Leadership Behaviours to Service Performance: Do Managers Make a Difference?" *Managing Service Quarterly* 5 (6), 1995. 26–31.

3. Smith. A. (2017). "Arizona Community Colleges Cope with State Disinvestment and Declining Enrollments." *Inside Higher Education*. January 27, 2017.

4. *Recommendation of the Ohio Higher Education Funding Commission*. (2014). Ohio Community Colleges.org. http://ohiocommunitycolleges.org/wp-content/uploads/2014/09/higheredufunding.pdf?x57939 (accessed August 4, 2017).

5. Smith. A. (2016). "Overtime Impact at 2-Year Colleges." *Inside Higher Education*. May 23, 2016.

6. Alfred, R. A. (2016). "Paradoxical Leadership." Strategic Horizon Network Colloquium. Pittsburgh. June 3, 2016.

7. Carl Haynes. Personal communication. March 25, 2017.

8. Carter, P., and Alfred, R. (1999). *Making Change Happen*. Ann Arbor, MI: Consortium for Community College Development.

9. Fullan, M. (1993). *Change Forces*. Philadelphia: Falmer Press.

10. Neff, T. J., and Citrin, J. M. (2005). *You're in Charge—Now What?* New York: Crown Publishing.

11. Watkins, M. D. (2013). *The First 90 Days*. Boston: Harvard Business School Publishing.

12. Schwartz, Ariel. (2011). "How Lessons from Toyota's Production Line Will Help Efficiently Rebuild New Orleans." *Fast Company*. June 29, 2011. https://www.fastcompany.com/1763849/how-lessons-toyotas-production-line-will-help-efficiently-rebuild-new-orleans (accessed August 4, 2017).

13. Mackey, J., and Sisodia, R. (2014). *Conscious Capitalism*. Boston: Harvard Business Review Press. 179.

14. Kouzes, J. M., and Posner, B. Z. (1995). *The Leadership Challenge*. San Francisco: Jossey-Bass.

15. Goleman, D. (1995). *Emotional Intelligence*. New York. Bantam Dell.

16. Katz, D. (2017). Personal communication. February 7, 2017.

17. Dweck. C. S. (2012). *Mindset: The New Psychology of Success*. New York: Ballantine Books.

18. Cameron, K. (2012). *Positive Leadership: Strategies for Extraordinary Performance*. San Francisco: Berrett-Koehler Publishers. 3.

19. Ibid., 2.

20. Ibid., 33–42.

21. Ibid., 39.

22. Rath, T., and Clifton, D. O. (2004). *How Full Is Your Bucket?* New York: Gallup Press.

23. Cameron. (2012). *Positive Leadership: Strategies for Extraordinary Performance*. 3.

24. Ibid., 54.

25. Ibid.

26. Ibid.

27. Association of Community College Trustees. (2016). "Trusteeship 101." *ACCT Quarterly*. Fall, 2016.

28. American Association of Community Colleges. (2015). *CEO Compensation Survey*. https://www.aacc.nche.edu/wp-content/uploads/2017/08/CEOSurvey_05012016.pdf.

29. Smith, A. (2016). "Many Community College Presidencies Are in Upheaval." *Inside Higher Ed*. May 20, 2016.

30. Association of Community College Trustees. (2016). "Trusteeship 101."

31. Ibid.

32. Sonnenfeld, J. A. (2002). "What Makes Great Boards Great." *Harvard Business Review*. September, 2002.

33. Newton, R. (2016). "HR Can't Change Company Culture by Itself." *Harvard Business Review*. November 2, 2016.

34. Murray, E. (2017). Personal communication. February 15, 2017.

35. Lencioni, P. (2002). *Five Dysfunctions of a Team: A Leadership Fable*. San Francisco: Jossey-Bass.

36. Patterson, K., Grenny, J., McMillan, R., and Switzler, A. (2012). *Crucial Conversations: Tools for Talking When Stakes Are High*. New York: McGraw-Hill.

37. Tushman, M. L., and Romanelli, E. (1985). "Organizational Evolution: A Metamorphosis Model of Convergence and Reorientation." In *Research in Organizational Behavior*, vol. 7, L. L. Cummings, and B. M. Staw (eds.): 171–222. Greenwich, CT: JAI Press.

38. Carter and Alfred. (1999). *Making Change Happen*.

39. Fullan. (1993). *Change Forces*. 39.

40. VanWagoner, R. J. (2004). "Influencing the Perception of Organizational Change in Community Colleges." *Community College Journal of Research and Practice* 28 (9), 2004. 715–27.

41. Alfred, R. L., Shults, C., Jaquette, O., and Strickland, S. (2009). *Community Colleges on the Horizon: Challenge, Choice, or Abundance*. Lanham, MD: Rowman & Littlefield. 144.

42. Ibid., 145.

43. Ulrich, D., and Ulrich, W. (2010). "Abundance Response: Focus People First on Meaning and Purpose." *Leadership Excellence*. August, 2010.

44. Lumina Foundation website. https://www.luminafoundation.org/todays-student-statistics (accessed November 11, 2017).

45. Goldrick-Rab, S., Richardson, J., and Hernandez, A. (2017). *Hungry and Homeless in College: Results of a National Study of Basic Needs Insecurity in Higher Education*. Madison: Wisconsin Hope Lab. March, 2017.

46. DeRionne Pollard. (2017). Personal communication. November 20, 2017.

47. Harris, Carla. *Here's How to Fix Culture*. Panel presentation at Fast Company Innovation Festival. October 25, 2017. New York.

48. Marcia Ballinger. (2017). Personal communication. November 12, 2017.

49. Williams, D. (2013). *Strategic Diversity Leadership*. Sterling, VA: Stylus Publishing. 194.

50. Ibid., 195.

51. Collins, J., and Porras, J. (1994). *Built to Last*. New York: HarperCollins.

Chapter Four

Building Colleges into Communities

When people are financially invested, they want a return. When people are emotionally invested, they want to contribute.

—Simon Sinek

As I was finishing my master's degree in community college administration, I was considering taking a job at a nearby community college. My doctoral advisor urged me to exercise caution. He feared that I might develop "bad habits" as a young professional in an organization with a dysfunctional culture. The notion of people shaping culture and culture shaping people has stuck with me throughout my career. A telltale characteristic of unhealthy cultures is elevated levels of employee disengagement with a critical mass of personnel focused on simply doing their job, but in a manner disconnected from the higher purpose of the enterprise.

In community colleges, the mission of student success can be personalized by individual faculty and staff helping students in the way they see fit, with varying levels of connection to the big picture. This variation can create unintended consequences of well-intended action. Best intentions can create uneven and disparate experiences for students if individual behavior is not guided by an overarching collective purpose of the organization.

In contrast, healthy cultures have an air of employee engagement and investment that permeates the organization. The organization may have ongoing pressure points and areas of conflict, but to an outsider coming in, the spirit and tenor of the place is positive and palpable. The sense of community shows through individuals equally committed to not letting their colleagues down and helping the college be successful in carrying out its mission. How does an organization increase employee engagement and a sense of community that leads to increased organizational performance? This chapter will explore several components of employee engagement with examples from

Mohawk Valley Community College (MVCC) and other colleges to set the stage for chapter 5, which focuses on organizational performance.

BUILDING TRUST THROUGH TRANSPARENCY

Transforming organizational culture is a daunting endeavor. A study by McKinsey and Company found that "companies are no more successful at overhauling their performance and organizational health than they were ten years ago. A particular blind spot seems to be the failure to involve frontline employees and their managers in the effort."[1] Involvement requires trust.

As presented in chapter 3, leaders can build trust through consistent behavior and decisions that send a message of authenticity and integrity. However, leaders are understandably challenged by the complexity and pace of change that make communication and trust building challenging. Disciplined, intentional effort is required to build employee engagement and attention to transparency and authenticity is essential.

Increasing Connection

Building connections is the key to building trust. Unfortunately, this work is increasingly harder in the modern workplace. As former United States surgeon general Vivek Murthy writes,

> There is good reason to be concerned about social connection in our current world. Loneliness is a growing health epidemic. We live in the most technologically connected age in the history of civilization, yet rates of loneliness have doubled since the 1980s. Today over 40 percent of adults in America report feeling lonely, and research suggests that the real number may well be higher.[2]

This epidemic of loneliness quietly weaves its way into the workplace every day. Loneliness is not only associated with poor health, but also "reduces task performance, limits creativity, and impairs other aspect of executive function such as reasoning and decision making." Humans are social creatures and often draw energy from interacting with others. A lack of interaction can drain energy from a person, leaving them with diminished capacity to deal with the stress and demands of their job. This can result in a sense of exhaustion and being overwhelmed, along with increased frustration at work. A related consequence to all of this is an increased lack of connection and perceptions of poor communication.

"Communication" often surfaces in organizational climate survey results, with lower-than-desired scores and comments calling for greater transparency in administrative matters. Leaders typically respond with "walk abouts" that accompany college-wide e-mails, posting information on webpages, town halls, and other opportunities for two-way communication through open forums on campus. This can feel like thankless work: no matter how much communication a leader puts forth, it is never enough. Regardless of how effective communication might be, the reality is that communication is work that never stops. Leaders cannot do enough to improve communication and trust throughout the organization.

Communication challenges can often be mitigated through visibility. Kris Duffy, president of Adirondack Community College, observes,

> The single most significant lever for a college president is being visible in both formal and informal settings. Walking around and saying "hello" to people on an informal basis builds a relationship that is not solely for the purpose of accomplishing a set agenda item. . . . Even when we disagree, a relationship outside the task will more times than not supersede negativity.[3]

Building this reservoir of goodwill before it is needed in trying times builds trust and creates pockets of stabilizers throughout the organization. However, increased visibility should not just be the task of the president, but should also include other senior leaders who need to get out of their office and "humanize" themselves to increase connections and expand trust through daily interactions in their own areas of responsibility as well as others. Colleges can pursue a variety of strategies, events, and programs that increase connections and build a stronger sense of community through consistent attention to the importance of this work. (See appendix B.)

Since increased communication can help build trust, new mechanisms must be continuously pursued. Advances in technology can seem overwhelming at times and create a fog of possibilities that are difficult to sort out and actually pursue. However, more cloud-based collaboration platforms offer new possibilities. One offering is the application of Workplace, by Facebook. Although it is completely contained within the organization, it looks and feels like Facebook. Workplace allows colleagues to interact via groups or chat, essentially offering the social network features in an organizational environment through postings, messaging, discussion boards, video, and other communication mechanisms that transcend the limited impact of overdone e-mail or static webpages.

Applications like Workplace go beyond traditional e-mail and webpages to create more effective communication strategies in an increasingly complex and fast-paced world. Although it is too early to gauge large-scale impact, the first-semester application of Workplace at MVCC has been successful. An e-mail invitation was sent to the 750 full- and part-time employees with instructions for joining Workplace by Facebook.

Within two weeks, more than 450 users activated their accounts, and, by the end of the first month, around 300 daily, active users were engaged in creating groups, posting, viewing posts, and sending messages to each other. Within a short time, Workplace created a new communication platform that allows a unique blend of formal and informal sharing among employees. Some colleges like St. Petersburg Community College have begun experimenting with the platform as a communication mechanism with and for students as well.

Alignment: Starting with Why

People generally like to be part of something greater than themselves. They want to make a difference, but with a majority of employees carrying out daily responsibilities in the narrow scope of a job description, the big picture can be hard to see. The challenge of helping everyone see, understand, and experience alignment between vision, mission, and strategic and departmental plans is a daunting task for leaders.

An instructor can readily draw a connection between classroom teaching and improving student success, but how does teaching connect to a strategic goal of developing community partnerships? It may be difficult to discern a connection between community partnerships that provide additional support services to help students succeed and classroom activity. At best, an instructor will be aware that support is in place, but may fail to connect the partnership to their teaching—let alone a departmental plan, the strategic plan, or mission of the college. Helping others connect the dots takes work.

Alignment is possible when statements and plans are recast into Simon Sinek's golden circle—the simple framework of *why, how,* and *what.* Sinek argues that ordinary companies focus on *what* they do and high-performing companies may add *how* they do what they do, but rarely crystallize why they do what they do. Extraordinary companies, like Apple, however, start with *why* they do *what* they do to inspire *how* they do and shape *what* it is in fact they do.[4]

The essence of the *why* for community colleges can be found in vision statements. A quick Internet search will yield numerous examples of vision statements in which community colleges recognize their potential to change or transform lives through learning. It is common for colleges to create a vision statement that goes on their website and into college publications but rarely do they create them in a way that communicates the *why* of that vision.

Extraordinary colleges find ways to leverage their vision statement into a sense of *why* they do what they do. Many colleges have developed vision statements that speak to what they aspire to be, a statement that draws them to the future. Others have vision statements that anchor them in the past, present, and future. Applying Sinek's golden circle to *why* community colleges do what they do can easily be translated to a college's stating, "We believe in the power of education to transform lives. Everything we do is focused on helping our students be successful to enable them to add value in the communities in which they live and work—ultimately adding to the quality of life in our region." This statement of vision speaks to *why* a college does what it does.

Most leaders know that common elements of organizational culture include shared values, norms, and beliefs of the personnel that work there. And yet, organizations are not often intentional enough about leveraging values and the stories that are part of the organizational narrative into the *why* and *how*. As leaders, we get caught up in *what* needs to get done in contrast to spending more of our time reinforcing the *why* to inform *how* things get done. Too great a focus on *what* needs to get done is shortsighted when it comes to shaping organizational culture.

What community colleges do is remarkably the same across the country, as the general purpose of these colleges creates a common organizational DNA. Despite our desire for distinctiveness, our programs and services have marginal variation that begins with *how* community colleges connect and *why* they exist to do *what* they do. This connection can be most frequently found in a meaningful statement of core values. Meaningful because, unfortunately, there is also not much variation in core value statements across community colleges.

Too many colleges have similar statements—for example, core values like learning, innovation, integrity, diversity, collaboration, sustainability, and other descriptors pepper community college websites across the country. Although it is clear that many leaders believe that culture is a primary factor in the success of a college, few institutions leverage values to propel employees to the higher purpose of the organization.

Values statements should be about action, not philosophy.[5] A few years ago, Mohawk Valley was updating its strategic plan and used the planning process to revisit our values statement. The charge to the design team focused on developing recommendations for a refined set of core values that would be distinct and not found at any other college. The team surveyed students, faculty, staff, and alumni to share stories about what makes MVCC unique and describe the core of what makes MVCC special.

The response was positive—more than two hundred stories. The team analyzed the stories and captured compelling phrases (without changing any words) and used them to develop a follow-up survey asking respondents to rank the phrases. The top four that emerged included these:

- Model the way.
- Inspire confidence.
- Encourage excellence.

- Embrace community.

These values are supported by sixteen action steps (four for each value) and they drive to the importance of doing the right thing for the right reasons in the right manner by modeling the way. They speak to providing the necessary support for our most vulnerable students by inspiring confidence (in a college where 73 percent of the first-time-ever-in-college population receives Pell Grants). They speak to maintaining high standards and challenging students by encouraging excellence. And they speak to embracing community, whether it be creating an inclusive campus environment and championing equity, welcoming the external community on campus through partnerships, or simply reflecting the community in different ways.

Creating core values unique to an institution opens a larger conversation about *how* people go about their work. The power of these values can be reinforced through "values moments" to start weekly staff meetings at the Cabinet, divisional, or departmental level, where members share a faculty, staff, or student story from the past week to bring one or more of the core values to life.

Mission statements are subject to the same fate as core value statements: they can often be mundane and duplicate one another across the national community college landscape. Boilerplate on themes like "meeting the diverse needs of the community by providing high-quality, accessible, affordable educational opportunities" is common among colleges regardless of size, history, or location.

Stories can be used to breathe life into mission statements by creating powerful illustrations about what a college is. A story might begin with a unique mission slant like this:

> Transformation College believes in the power of education to transform lives through wraparound service for our students in partnership with the community.
>
> A student named Dennis recently experienced what a college like Transformation can do. Dennis is a military veteran who was unemployed, filing for bankruptcy, and going through a divorce. He lost his car and his home and was experiencing health issues along with food insecurity. Transformation's community resource specialist connected him with local food banks and temporary housing that gave him the stability to get his own apartment. She also helped him secure part-time employment, an unlimited bus pass, pro bono legal counsel to help with his divorce, and financial counseling to help with his bankruptcy.
>
> He remains enrolled full-time, is doing well, and is registered for next semester, and remains on track for his degree.

Dennis's story paints a clear picture of the college and how mission, vision, and values connect with culture to achieve a mission of transforming lives.

Alignment between declaration and action is a powerful lever for shaping organizational culture. It requires time on clarifying the *why*, *what*, and *how* a college goes about its work into an aligned set of statements that flow together and anchor staff to the big picture. An aligned organizational narrative must be reinforced time and again with powerful stories and examples that bring mission, vision, and values to life by illuminating actions and connecting them to how and why they were done. Alignment creates clarity and sets the foundation for employee engagement.

CASTING IS EVERYTHING

Culture is about people. For leaders choosing to transform culture, no larger lever exists than the way in which an organization identifies, attracts and welcomes new cast members. It starts with recruitment and how people are brought on board in an organization. New members are like fresh thread to be carefully woven into the ever-evolving tapestry that is the culture of an organization.

To cast people in the right roles, intentional effort must be made to clearly define roles and responsibilities in the structure of an organization. This is an example of where organizational discipline is important: it takes time and attention to develop a comprehensive understanding of organizational structure. If an organization wants to create consistent behavior across programs and services in ways that align with core values, values need to be explicitly stated in every position description.

How else can staff be held accountable for behavior that is explicitly stated in the form of values by the organization? And yet most organizations do not embed core values in positions to create consistent behavior that can drive culture. When a vacancy occurs, the natural instinct for supervisors is to fill it as soon as possible in order that work can continue. Taking the time to infuse clarity into a role by refining the position description, affirming expected behaviors and values, and clarifying the current attributes and skills required can advance the organization through each and every position.

Many colleges run into obstacles attracting and hiring talent in the form of cumbersome hiring processes resulting from decades of compromises, all made in the spirit of shared governance. A routine search committee process is employed with the highest of ideals, comprised of staff with a vested interest in filling each position with the best candidate. Multiple perspectives are important, so committees have at least five, seven, or sometimes more faculty and staff serving on the committee. With large search committees, simply the logistics of getting calendars together for meetings and interviews can extend the search process. It is not uncommon for colleges to take four or more months to fill vacancies.

Extended search processes negatively impact cultural transformation by inhibiting the ability of colleges to keep top talent out of the hands of organizations with more efficient hiring processes. Colleges with healthy cultures are staffed with employees who understand that efficient and well-designed hiring processes attract top talent with the character, initiative, and passion to put core values into action.

In addition to the glacial pace of search processes with large committees, membership can greatly influence a search. Peers sitting on a search committee charged with hiring a future colleague may argue that they will have to work with the person on a daily basis, but yet they will not be responsible for issuing progressive discipline or reprimanding the low-performing employee if things go wrong. A committee empowered to identify candidates in preferred order to a supervisor, only to discover that someone other than the top candidate is selected, will eventually communicate its displeasure to colleagues.

Search committees can also include individuals who bring personal bias—subtle and not so subtle—into the process. Whether self-interest ensures the successful candidate will not raise the bar too much and make coworkers work harder, or subtle bias against gender, racial, ethnic, disability, or another demographic, one or more narrow-minded, disconnected committee members involved in a search can poison the process.

Years ago, I witnessed a supervisor aim to hire the best talent for a position only to be confronted with a search committee filled with members who were clearly looking to hire talent for future union leadership regardless of qualifications and experience for the job. I have also worked with supervisors coming from the private sector commenting on their first hiring experience in a college culture by asking, "Is it always this hard to hire somebody? I used to just place an ad, interview the candidates myself, and hire the best person. This seems like we're overthinking it." The existing culture has a significant influence on hiring processes, which in the long term also have a significant influence on the shape and form of the future culture.

Fortunately, alternatives exist. Tulsa Community College, for example, developed a matrix with key characteristics of their ideal employee and uses it to hire, develop, and promote personnel within the organization.[6] Other colleges engage leaders in the hiring and development process in carefully crafted ways. Jackson College adds an important step to the hiring process with their senior leaders to ensure continuity of culture. The Leadership Council (president's senior leadership team) interviews the final candidate for all full- and part-time positions after reviewing materials and recommendations from the work of screening committees. The purpose of the interview is to explore the extent to which finalists align with the values, beliefs, and behavioral norms of the institution.[7] This step is an example of the intentionality and discipline required to shape organizational culture. Before candidates are hired, the senior leadership team engages them in a conversation about culture that provides clarity about the nature of work at the college and what will be expected of them to contribute and succeed.

A middle ground to consider is a process that incorporates elements of multiple processes, often referred to as a *serial interview*—a sequence of interviews that allow for multiple engagements with candidates, each from a different perspective. Rather than the narrow lens of a single supervisor or the complexity of a large search committee, a small screening committee can effectively manage a serial interview process. To advance the hiring process, three people can align their calendars more quickly than a larger group. Identifying individuals who can contribute to the process in unique ways gives the serial interview process energy and value.

Rather than five to seven people struggling to align time for interviews and meetings and review of resumes and support materials, a committee of three can easily manage all of these elements. Someone beyond the committee can provide the campus tour; someone in human resources can review benefits with the candidates; time can be arranged to meet with the department and colleagues who will be working with the successful candidate; and other personnel can meet on the front or back end of the candidate's time on campus for an informal conversation.

The supervisor can follow up with a "360 conversation" with everyone involved in the process to discuss candidates and compare interactions and impressions. This process can provide the supervisor with enhanced perspective and insight to make an informed hiring decision without the political pressure of a large committee or an elongated process that may lose top candidates along the way.

Welcome Home

In the modern multigenerational workplace, connectivity with new employees is critical. A definitive culture with comprehensible norms and expectations for behavior is more important than ever. Without it, broad cultural impact on new members is lost to the depths of internal subcultures. Connecting new members with the tangible benefits of working at a community college like payroll, healthcare, retirement, vacation and sick leave is important to make individuals feel safe and secure. Connecting new members with intangible benefits of working at a community college, like being part of changing lives and strengthening the local community while working in a professional, high-energy environment, can make individuals feel inspired.

At an administrative roundtable meeting a few years ago at Mohawk Valley, the monthly discussion topic began with a prompt: "What do you do with a new employee on their first day?" The groups inventoried all the different steps they took as supervisors on the first day. We collected all the input and summarized it in a four-page, single-spaced document. My favorite reaction from one supervisor was, "This is a solid list. I've done all of these things with new employees on the first day . . . just never all of them with the same employee." That statement brought to the fore the reality that we did not have a consistent process for onboarding new employees.

The Human Resources Office provided a benefits overview and facilitated the necessary paperwork. We had a New Employee Orientation (NEO) experience that had limited impact because it was conducted twice a year for incoming cohorts of employees in August and January. And supervisors were generally left to their own devices to onboard new employees. What emerged from the roundtable discussion was a "Start Right Program" at Mohawk Valley. It's a comprehensive checklist with reminders about how we want new employees to feel and step-by-step intentions in the onboarding process. (See appendix C.) For example, the Start Right Program principles are as follows:

> While nearly every position requires special elements with regard to orientation, certain information items and actions are essential for all new employees to get started in the most positive and productive manner possible. The following principles guide the Start Right Program by making each new employee feel like they are:
>
> - welcomed to the college,
> - part of a team and belong to a thriving learning community,
> - working with an emotionally intelligent supervisor that supports and cares about them and their success,
> - provided with the tools and resources to fulfill core job responsibilities,
> - comfortable and confident in their position from their very first day on the job, and
> - off to a productive and meaningful start to their career at MVCC. [8]

The Start Right Program provides supervisors with guidance for necessary onboarding steps that begin two weeks prior to an employee's first day. Some elements may seem simple, but even simple actions are often left to chance, and yet, discipline is critical to shaping and nurturing culture in all corners of an organization. Key steps include, but are not limited to the following:

1. Blocking out time on the supervisor's calendar on the first day, the first couple of days, and periodically throughout the first six months to create time for check-ins;
2. Preparing the workspace, account access, and other necessary resources for the new employee to create a welcoming environment for getting started;

3. Assigning a mentor or a resource person on the first day; and
4. Creating a calendar for the first week of human resources paperwork, meetings, and training to optimize use of time while keeping the schedule light and engaging so as not to be overwhelming. [9]

Recognizing that onboarding could be much more meaningful through a college-wide, supervisor-led program made it possible to rethink our New Employee Orientation (NEO) program. What used to be a long day full of human resources reminders, group tours of campus, and stale review of policies and procedures, has been replaced by a tight three-hour experience that is engaging and meaningful. Our primary design principles for NEO are to "love 'em up" and "get 'em connected."

Offered in August and January, we ask participants to complete the Gallup StrengthsFinder prior to the NEO session, which starts with an icebreaker followed by a thirty-minute introduction to Strengths. Participants are then joined for lunch by the President's Cabinet, who briefly introducing themselves—not only by sharing their responsibilities at the college, but also by describing how they use one of their top five strengths in their daily work.

Lunch is followed by a fifteen-minute video history of the college that connects new hires to a Mohawk Valley narrative to which they will write the next chapter. The NEO workshop closes with the vice presidents each telling a story that exemplifies a core value of the college to amplify *why* and *how* the college goes about its collective work. The "Start Right Program" and redesigned NEO have been critical to increasing the sense of alignment and belonging to continue evolving the culture at the college.

Incorporating the Gallup StrengthsFinder into our NEO has had a powerful effect on our ability to infuse Strengths throughout the organization. After nearly six years of incorporating Strengths into NEO, more than 75 percent of all full-time employees have taken the StrengthsFinder assessment. Nine out of ten Fortune 500 companies use the StrengthsFinder in some manner with their employees. [10]

Having its roots in positive psychology, Strengths reinforces a growth mind-set that connects people and encourages them to use their strengths by understanding themselves and their coworkers better through the vocabulary of Strengths. At Mohawk Valley, the Strengths effort has spilled over into our one-credit College Success Seminar required for all of our students. It has taken several years, but finding levers to weave Strengths into MVCC's culture has helped create a common language for some instructors and many staff and added a positive element to the workplace while laying a foundation for students to explore their own strengths.

ENGAGING ROLES

In *The Truth about Employee Engagement*, Patrick Lencioni states, "Employees who find fulfillment in their jobs are going to work with more enthusiasm, passion, and attention to quality than their counterparts who do not, mostly because they develop a sense of ownership and pride in what they are doing." An organization that makes employee engagement a priority will differentiate itself as a premier employer and experience a substantial increase in employee retention, productivity, and positive evolution in culture.[11]

Engagement starts with hiring the right people in the right roles and creating conditions for them to contribute in meaningful ways. Sisodia, Sheth, and Wolfe echo this notion by stating, "Organizational energy is created and released when an organization's people are emotionally and intellectually excited by the firm's vision and values. One of the most important tasks of a leader is to mobilize this energy and then focus it on the achievement of meaningful goals."[12]

Releasing organizational energy through meaningful work requires a consistent supervisory culture among managers to have a broad impact on culture. If the idea of assigning, shaping, and supporting meaningful work is left to individual managers without an overarching strategy, cultural transformation is not likely. According to Gallup, organizations suffer from a 70 percent variance in engagement based on the influence of managers.[13]

Leaders need help to give managers the tools to help employees see their work as part of a larger whole. With tools in hand, supervisors need to manage what Lencioni calls the three root causes of a miserable job:

1. *Anonymity versus visibility*—Employees need to be seen by their supervisors and colleagues as participants in an environment that recognizes that they are more than a worker; they are an individual. If employees feel anonymous, their level of engagement and fulfillment is lowered and turnover is likely to increase. Employees need to feel seen, respected, cared for, and appreciated.
2. *Irrelevance versus meaning*—If employees are unable to see meaning and purpose in their work, engagement levels plummet. The difference between someone who finds meaning in work compared to a worker who finds negligible meaning is tangibly evident in their demeanor, interactions, attendance, productivity, and overall attitude. Meaning is important.
3. *Ambiguity and measurement*—Without clarity of expectations, individuals are left to their own devices to determine the extent to which they are successful or, at the very least, contributing and adding value in some way. To increase employee engagement, supervisors need to

clearly define expectations and the measurements for success to let employees know what they are expected to do. Employees need clarity and they need to know what success looks like.[14]

Addressing root causes of a poor job environment and creating a community of great people in clearly defined roles doing meaningful work requires that supervisors pay attention, know employees as individuals, and fully engage. Gallup has an ongoing Q12 survey to monitor employee engagement throughout the world across industry sectors and the data show lapses in every sector. In their ongoing study of workplace engagement, Gallup reports that only 30 percent of the current workforce indicate that they feel engaged in their work.[15] Using tools like the Gallup Q12 along with engaged supervisors who are trained and committed to employee engagement can have a positive impact on workplace culture.

Effective Governance

Employee engagement extends beyond the individual job. It involves the collective work of shared governance, which is a hallmark of the academic workplace. Shared governance is an accreditation standard and yet varies from institution to institution based on organizational culture. It can be a tricky thing, requiring a delicate dance between top-down and bottom-up strategies.

Some colleges have elaborate Planning and Governance Offices staffed with a director and support staff to manage meetings, calendars, initiatives, and minutes of numerous committees, whose members are determined jointly by union leadership and administration. In stark contrast, other colleges have college-wide councils performing mostly symbolic roles in shared governance. Something like a Teaching and Learning Council may be in place, but not approve curricula because the president eliminated the curriculum committee after feeling that the liberal arts faculty were creating unnecessary barriers and delays in curriculum approval for career and technical programs.

Years ago, Metropolitan Community College charged a yearlong design team with creating a streamlined alternative curriculum approval process (with no committee), which produced a new process based on a ten-step checklist of best practices that became the new way and remains to this day.

Rudimentary steps are necessary if governance is to contribute to cultural vitality. Roles, responsibilities, and structure need to be clarified. Nomenclature is important too, as some colleges have failed to draw distinctions between a committee, a council, a workgroup, a team, a task force, or other formally titled entity that carries out interdepartmental or cross-functional work. Defining the role and scope of organizational units provides clarity and boundaries for a robust governance structure.

Sunny Cooke, president of Mira Costa Community College near San Diego, works within the governance process legislated in California.

> We call it participatory or collegial governance in contrast to shared governance. This creates a distinction between input and decision-making because accountability and responsibility are not equally shared by constituent members. Collegial governance ensures that stakeholders are at the table for earnest discussion so that diverse perspectives and ideas can be considered. [16]

Role clarity can build trust that helps groups to perform more efficiently. I have seen college senates linger in the mire of thick committee by-laws—spending hours on inane wordsmithing changes and refinements to by-laws in contrast to tackling real issues in the organization. Replacing by-laws with simple, one-page charters can increase focus and efficiency by clarifying group membership and purpose.

An additional step to add energy to any system of shared governance is to establish a mechanism to strengthen the connection between the senior leadership team (Leadership Council, President's Cabinet, etc.) and leadership (steering or executive committee, etc.) of the primary governance body (College Council, College Senate or Assembly, etc.).

At Mohawk Valley, an annual retreat—usually a half-day meeting during lunch and an afternoon—provides a forum to jointly reflect on the past year and assess shared governance work at the college. The conversation naturally transitions to a review of the strategic plan and annual plan for developing shared priorities in the coming year. Discussion invariably surfaces successes, gains, and best practices as well as opportunities for improvement. Most importantly, however, open and candid dialogue builds trust among all involved.

Employee involvement in governance is a hallmark of a healthy culture. Yet despite its obvious importance, many institutions are not aware of the extent of employee involvement in governance. This results in the often-heard charge that "the same people are involved in everything." To counter this common cultural habit requires intentionality and discipline that can be part of an inventory of the extent to which each full-time employee is engaged in governance or interdepartmental work—a summary of capacity, in a way.

This would be difficult at larger institutions, but it can be scaled by campus, division, or department. A simple inventory can be created and populated with the membership and engagement of each employee in various institutional groups and initiatives. The next level of analysis would be the extent to which those assignments are placed and leveraged. If some of the most talented employees are toiling in tangential, low-impact groups, something needs to change.

Capacity can be enhanced by exchanging low-impact assignments of high performers for high-impact assignments. For example, a faculty leader serving on four or five low-impact committees could drop three of those assignments and become more actively involved in a Student Success Council or other significant group. Assessing the extent to which college service commitments of talented members are aligned with college priorities can greatly accelerate results throughout the institution.

Engaging in the Life of the College

Employee engagement is greatly influenced by the daily work of individuals in their regular job responsibilities and their participation in shared governance. Perhaps an even greater accelerator for engagement is employee participation in new initiatives. Ideally, most employees want to have an impact and to be connected to something beyond their normal workgroup. The simultaneous pursuit of multiple initiatives is commonplace in most colleges and provides the groundwork for engagement through the organizational need for capacity.

Strategic plans, for example, with numerous goals and objectives, along with initiatives related to community needs, grant programs, and mandates from government agencies, present opportunities for employees to engage in the life of the college. As illustrated by the case studies in chapter 2, strategic plans can play a significant role in transforming culture. The face of change moderates as faculty and staff encounter new information and are exposed to outside perspectives.

Active participation in planning connects employees to goals and objectives in the finished plan leading ultimately to engagement in initiatives that advance the plan. Engagement continues to increase as employees feel a sense of ownership of initiatives they helped implement, leading to further engagement in planning and continuous improvement.

Another strategy for increasing employee engagement is the use of process-improvement teams or system-design teams. If the timing isn't right for a new president to launch a full-scale strategic planning process, an alternative approach might be to create design teams to examine major systems such as

- student intake
- student support
- hiring systems
- professional development
- employee recognition

• adjunct faculty support

Co-chairs for each team could be selected with an eye to expand leadership opportunities and members who are not always selected for college-wide initiatives. Charters directing the teams to make "bold and daring" recommendations to improve the system they are studying can set the tone, as the groups go about assessing internal systems and benchmarking against best practices.

A key element in the process is to have teams make draft recommendations and meet with senior leaders and the functional-area vice president to shape final recommendations together. This process can create doable action steps that allow for recommendations to be implemented almost to the letter while getting inclusive change strategies in motion. In most cases, the experience increases the engagement level of participants and prompts engagement in future organizational initiatives.

DEVELOPMENT AND ENRICHMENT

While many colleges use professional development to build capacity for new initiatives, it is often overlooked as a lever to shape organizational culture over time. Unfortunately, professional development (PD) is too easily identified as an early casualty during difficult budget deliberations. Cultural transformation requires envisioning professional development as an avenue for setting conditions for creative collisions to occur, fostering new ways of thinking, and exposing the organization to new ideas. If private-sector businesses allocate a percentage of their annual budget to product research and development, why can't community colleges do the same with PD? For as little as 1 percent of the overall operating budget, a college can develop a robust array of professional development offerings.

Larger institutions have the resources to establish centers of excellence (i.e., Teaching and Learning, Professional Development, etc.), while smaller institutions may have a faculty member on partial release time to coordinate training and workshops. Other institutions use professional development committees or enrichment councils, or a combination of resources, to coordinate activities.

Regardless of approach, employee engagement is promoted and nurtured by resourcing and operating a comprehensive professional development program over a period of years. Primary populations include new and mid-career employees, teaching faculty, frontline staff, mid-level managers, and administrators. Programming includes teaching and learning, student success, customer-service leadership, assessment, equity, and many others. Essential in professional development is creating an infrastructure with mechanisms and support to deliver a diverse and comprehensive array of high-quality programming throughout the year.

Leaders should not underestimate the importance of professional development in cultural transformation. While implementing all elements of a comprehensive PD program may not be feasible at all colleges, meeting the culture where it is and building quality programming one piece at a time over several years makes it more possible. Consider these items:

- *Institutes, Professional Development, and In-Service Days*: Many colleges have set-aside days each academic term for workshops and training relevant to operating needs. When training is leveraged with focus and direction, a critical mechanism can be realized for shaping organizational culture. Experiences can be provided to expose employees to new ideas, spark critical conversations, and advance the collective thinking on important topics and issues.
- *New Employee Orientation*: Focus programming on connecting employees to the *why* and *how* of the organization, leaving the *what* to be addressed more specifically by supervisors.
- *New Faculty Institute*: Create cohort-based programming for the first-year new faculty experience. Weekly, biweekly, or monthly formats with or without a class release can focus teaching along with connecting new faculty with support services throughout the college.
- *Sabbaticals*: Utilize sabbaticals for faculty and administrators to go beyond the standard objective of personal renewal and align sabbatical projects with college needs and initiatives.
- *Tech Academy*: Provide full-time faculty with a one-course release to pursue a personal learning agenda and expand their skill set with educational technologies. Create faculty learning communities around hybrid/blended course development, open educational resources, or other technology-enhanced formats.
- *Return to Industry Internships*: Provide faculty with a stipend for participation in a summer learning program in the local workforce. The emphasis is placed on meeting with employers and visiting workplaces to gain insight into the modern workplace as a means for enhancing their teaching with current examples in the field.
- *Assessment Academies*: Provide faculty with time and support to review assessment results and refine action plans to improve student success.
- *Leadership Academy*: Create a cohort-based program to develop leadership skills based on the principle of leading at all levels from anywhere in the organization.
- *Adjunct Faculty*: Create opportunities for the development of adjunct faculty with a focus on ongoing orientation, engagement in curriculum and assessment results, and exposure in active learning strategies. Adjunct

faculty professional development is an important component to building a culture of student success.

* *Wellness and Enrichment*: Focus on the whole person by recognizing personal health and wellness can increase job performance. Providing visible and accessible support to employees through exposure to enrichment opportunities can increase job satisfaction and engagement.
* *Travel in Teams*: Although counter to traditional thinking in many colleges, sending more than one member to state and national conferences can yield a strong return on the investment. Not only does this approach expand the learning that occurs and increase the energy brought back into the institution, it also provides a great opportunity to strengthen relationships and build memories among members through all the unscheduled time traveling, waiting at the airport, and going to dinner.

RETHINKING EVALUATION AND REWARDS

While hiring is all about casting new members, culture and community are all about performance. Evaluation and rewards are critical levers for increasing performance. As public entities, community colleges may have to become creative with rewards that positively influence employee engagement. Pay for performance is not easily translated from the private sector to the public sector. Merit pay in union environments requires caution, willing labor partners, and clear criteria in purpose and execution.

Not only can evaluation processes shape individual and organizational performance, but they can greatly influence the culture as well. Like students craving feedback on their assignments, faculty and staff benefit from constructive, strengths-based, and timely feedback delivered in strategic and emotionally intelligent ways. It is more likely that someone will underperform if they are unclear on what they are supposed to be doing or if they have no idea how their supervisor thinks they are doing.

Good culture is nurtured by people feeling safe and confident in their roles that are defined by clear and up-to-date job descriptions that promote the organizational core values. This is complemented by supervisors providing regular feedback—at a minimum a midyear "check-in" in addition to the annual evaluation—and perhaps even a periodic 360 feedback review from some of their colleagues.

As a natural complement to evaluation, promotion processes represent an important form of rewards. An important balance needs to be struck between complex and burdensome peer-review processes for promotions that can be unduly influenced by technicalities and politics, and simplified processes that are reliant on the opinion of a single supervisor. Promotion processes with standards and criteria that prevent selection from devolving into a rubber stamp give recognition more meaning. Processes with checks and balances that include meaningful progression with clear criteria can help make promotions an important part of a larger rewards system.

In addition to pay and promotions, time can be another reward to increase employee engagement. The gift of time creates capacity for employees to pursue additional responsibilities while maintaining some level of work-life balance. Release time is a common reward employed for faculty recognition. Whether it be a semester or yearlong sabbatical or a course release from teaching, faculty who receive release time are more often than not invigorated by the reward of time. Faculty returning from sabbatical can often be heard to say, "I had no idea how burned out I was!" and "It was great to be away, but I am so excited to be back—I have so many new ideas, I can't wait to get going!" The gift of time creates space for faculty to refresh, balance, focus, and renew themselves, which combine to create the conditions for increased engagement.

Staff do not often have access to release time or sabbaticals the way faculty do. However, one approach with similar benefits is affording staff the opportunity for flextime. Although this is a common summer practice at many colleges, the stress of daily life makes flextime a subtle, but potentially effective, reward that can increase employee engagement and be considered for year-round availability.

A primary challenge with implementing flextime is rooted in the principle of equality in many campus cultures—why does the admissions office have access to flextime year-round while the business office only has access in summer? Allowing for variation in work schedules is common in areas like events, facilities, public safety, and athletics to accommodate institutional needs. But variation is meaningless when considering flextime from an employee perspective where, if one unit can make it work, why shouldn't flextime be allowed year-round for all units, as long as office coverage is managed?

Like so many other parts of creating a sense of community in a coherent culture, successfully implementing flextime depends on the ability of supervisors to do so in a thoughtful and reasonable manner throughout the institution. Flextime is a clear indicator of employer recognition of the importance of balancing personal- and work-life responsibilities and an important symbol of employee valuation.

COMPREHENSIVE RECOGNITION

Employees who feel valued exhibit higher levels of satisfaction and engagement in their work and the life of the college. Leaders may feel that there is only so much they can do to recognize employees because recognition takes on different meaning for individuals.

Recognition can take many forms, including increased pay, awards presented at ceremonies, handwritten notes, compliments in front of others at meetings, gifts, "who made my day" programs, individual praise from a supervisor, selection into a professional development program, service on a major institutional initiative, invitation to attend a conference, or numerous other forms that have varied levels of meaning and value depending on the employee. Variation in value makes recognition difficult to get right.

Like most colleges, Mohawk Valley has an annual awards luncheon to close the academic year. During my first year as president, I read more than 130 names in the span of forty-five minutes for the years of service recognition. Batches of employees in five-year cohorts had their names read aloud as they proceeded to the stage for a group photo. I asked an employee recognition design team to reimagine service recognition at the college.

Based on the group's recommendation, service recognition has become more personalized and now occurs throughout the year in individual ceremonies. As close to the honoree's anniversary date as possible, I join the functional-area vice president and supervisor and spend a few minutes with each employee to recognize them for ten, fifteen, or more years of service. We use that time to give each employee a framed certificate and share stories that illustrate how much their dedication and hard work is appreciated. The mini-ceremonies are shared in our daily communication "MVCC Today" so that colleagues can join in and share their own stories of appreciation and gratitude.

Awards can be designed to reinforce organizational culture by aligning with core values or a theme that resonates with the college. MVCC athletics mascot is "Mo" the Hawk—we're the Hawks—so several years ago, the employee recognition design team recommended going beyond our existing SUNY Chancellor and MVCC Excellence Awards to create a series of Hawks that Soar! Awards. As a result, we have the following:

- Pride of the Hawk—Staff Excellence in Service (quarterly)
- Heart of the Hawk—Faculty Excellence in Teaching (quarterly)
- Wings of the Hawk—A pay-it-forward team or department service award each semester
- Eye of the Hawk—Excellence in Assessment (annual)
- Altitude Award—Excellence in Innovation (annual)
- Aeries Award—Excellence in Community Service (annual)

The Hawks that Soar! Awards are important symbols that remind us that all employees are Hawks and are bound together in the mission of the institution. They are all peer-nominated to incorporate and reinforce the power of gratitude and appreciation throughout the culture.

Another important recognition is that for retirees. Retirement was not clearly defined at MVCC; some employees would "retire" at sixty-five and others would simply "resign" from their position and walk away with no formal recognition by the college. Retirement is a life moment that should not go without recognition or definition.

An employee recognition design team was asked to develop a definition for retirement with the result that retirement was defined as being fifty-five years or older with ten or more years of service with retirees receiving their choice of a Harvard chair, rocker, or lamp. In addition, clearly defined criteria for emeritus faculty and administrator and distinguished retiree (technical and hourly staff) have helped to visibly recognize and celebrate long and significant careers for individuals.

While having an array of awards is important, the selection process requires discipline and attention. The selection process should include checks and balances and necessary vetting. For employees to place stock in a recognition program, each recipient needs to be a deserving recipient.

I have a clear memory of occasions on which recognizing the wrong award recipient had a negative impact on college culture. Years ago, when I received negative feedback on a peer-nominated award recipient, I asked the supervisor responsible for writing a strong support letter for a negative employee. The supervisor responded by saying, "I know the individual is not a very nice person and has a negative impact on everybody, but I hoped the nomination might turn things around."

Recognition processes can be compromised if not carried out with care and attention. They should reinforce an alignment between the vision, mission, and values of the organization and the criteria and process for selection, which should be abundantly clear to all employees. Recognition should celebrate achievement and promote habits that model what the organization looks like at its best.

CELEBRATION AND TRADITION

Beyond strengthening interpersonal bonds, celebrations and tradition are important elements to building a sense of community within an organizational culture. To a large extent, they are among the most visible symbols in culture—emblems that everyone can point to that say, "This is who we are." Part of thought and action by high-performing organizations in embedding celebrations into the culture.[17] Once identified, the frequency and quality of celebrations and traditions should be considered.

A college's annual calendar of events reveals many of its traditions. The academic year lends itself to a wonderfully consistent rhythm of tradition. Convocation, the first day and week of classes each semester, midterms, final exams, lunches and dinners celebrating accomplishments of students and employees, cultural events, fundraisers, graduation, and more—all comprise the comforting regularity that comes with working at a college. If celebrations and traditions are not treated as levers to influence culture and increase employee engagement, leaders are missing a significant opportunity.

Traditions vary by college from large galas and dinner dances to departmental gatherings. Like many colleges, MVCC holds a biannual "Celebration of Success" at the end of the fall and spring semesters. It typically goes 4–6 p.m. on a Tuesday or Wednesday during the week of graduation. Everyone gets a drink ticket, an array of heavy hors d'oeuvres, and typical reception food.

The event allows employees to connect and enjoy each other's company in a relaxed environment with music, food, and drink while highlights from the past semester at the college rotate on a large screen in the main area. The highlight of the event is the basket raffle involving baskets created and donated by roughly twenty-five college departments. Participants get two free tickets with the option to purchase additional tickets. Winners are called toward the end of the event. The basket raffle raises between $1,000 and $1,500 for local charities and promotes the college as a good "corporate citizen" in the community.

Another tradition at many colleges is a service day or mechanism to get employees together in the community for the benefit of a worthy cause. It can reinforce a sense of unity and shared purpose among colleagues—all while providing a memorable experience.

Team MVCC performs that role at Mohawk Valley. A small group of employees identify major community events (e.g., Relay for Life, Making Strides Against Breast Cancer, and other 5K run/walk events, etc.) as well as ad hoc fundraisers or volunteer opportunities. Employees register to participate, and if they donate to the MVCC Foundation annual campaign and participate in three of the annual Team MVCC events, they receive a small gift as a "4-Runner" for completing events.

Team MVCC typically raises more than $25,000 annually for outside community organizations. Community service and participation with colleagues from work increases a sense of well-being and supports employee engagement.

STAYING CONNECTED

Tending to the career trajectory of employees is an important component of managing employee engagement. New employees typically arrive on campus with their interview face—eyes wide open, ready for action, and willing to do anything, for any reason, and at any time![18] Along the way a portion of employees experience disengagement. Although some may eventually reengage, a number of employees actively disengage toward the end of their career.

Feeling it is too late in life to find a new career, they have little choice but to stick it out in a job for which they have lost passion and in an organization from which they feel disconnected. This profile stands in stark contrast to employees who gain momentum throughout their careers and are involved in numerous initiatives right up to the day they retire.

Beyond the obvious financial benefits to the budgetary bottom line, retirement incentives can serve as a catalyst for cultural transformation by changing the dynamics and actors involved in the work of the college. Some leaders shy away from retirement incentives because "employees you want to go don't take them and the ones that take the incentive are the ones you don't want to go." Although that may be true in some cases, strong hiring and onboarding systems will fill gaps in areas losing critical talent and maximize opportunities to fill vacancies where new energy is needed.

Retirements can create cracks and fissures in culture through change in players and relationships. One way to minimize the impact of transitions is a strong retiree recognition and emeritus program that includes regular retiree events. Some colleges have programs such as an annual retiree brunch to bring retirees back to campus, allow them time to reconnect, and provide an update on initiatives and happenings at the college. This approach keeps retirees connected, engaged, and a phone call away if assistance is needed.

REFLECTIONS ON ENGAGEMENT

Organizations with a culture of trust have the basis for conditions that foster a culture of employee engagement. Shared vision, purpose, and core values embedded in intentionally crafted hiring and onboarding processes, engage employees in the culture of the institution from their first interaction with the organization. Clearly defined roles, responsibilities, and expectations reinforce engagement through meaningful work day in and day out.

Opportunities to engage in effective governance structures and larger college initiatives expand the perceptual field of employees and connect them to units and staff throughout the organization. Robust professional development coupled with meaningful feedback, rewards, and recognition, along with celebrations and traditions, create an emotionally intelligent workplace with all the attributes of community and a hallmark of an engaged culture.

NOTES

1. Reich, A., and Yocarini, L. (2017). "The People Power of Transformations." February, 2017. http://www.mckinsey.com/business-functions/organization/our-insights/the-people-power-of-transformations (accessed August 6, 2017).

2. Murthy, V. (2017). "Work and the Loneliness Epidemic. *Harvard Business Review.* September, 2017. https://hbr.org/cover-story/2017/09/work-and-the-loneliness-epidemic.

3. Ibid.

4. Kris Duffy. (2017). Personal communication. July 13, 2017.

5. Sinek, S. (2009). *Start with Why: How Great Leaders Inspire Everyone to Action.* New York: Penguin Group.

6. Ric Baser. (2014). Personal communication. February 6, 2014.

7. Phelan, D. J. (2016). *Unrelenting Change, Innovation, and Risk: Forging the Next Generation of Community Colleges.* Lanham, MD: Rowman & Littlefield.

8. Mohawk Valley Community College Start Right Program.

9. Ibid.

10. Gray, E. (2015). "The XQ Factor." *Time Magazine.* July 22, 2015. 40–46.

11. Lencioni, P. (2007). *The Truth about Employee Engagement.* San Francisco: Jossey-Bass. 224.

12. Sisodia, R., Sheth, J., and Wolfe, D. B. (2007). *Firms of Endearment.* Upper Saddle River, NJ: Wharton School Publishing, 201.

13. "Employee Engagement." Gallup News. http://www.gallup.com/topic/employee_engagement.aspx (accessed May 14, 2017).

14. Lencioni. (2007). *The Truth about Employee Engagement.*

15. "Employee Engagement." Gallup News.

16. Sunita Cooke. (2017). Personal communication. June 4, 2017.

17. Sisodia, R., Sheth, J., and Wolfe, D. B. (2007). *Firms of Endearment.* Upper Saddle River, NJ: Wharton School Publishing, 85.

18. Pastizzo, F., and Pastizzo, S. (2008). *Warming Up the Workplace.* Norwood, NY: Warming Up the Workplace.

Chapter Five

Today's Cultural Imperative

A Culture of Inquiry

The price of light is less than the cost of darkness.
    —Arthur C. Nielsen, Market Researcher and Founder of ACNielsen

When I was a graduate student at the University of Michigan, my doctoral advisor told me, "If you want to go into community colleges, you should start in institutional research." I asked, "Why there instead of student affairs or academics?" He quickly responded, "Because community colleges don't know much about themselves and you'll learn the whole organization from the inside out because everyone is going to need data." That was 1990 and he was profoundly correct, if not prescient.

Institutional research was a great place for me to start and I learned a lot about the community college enterprise in a short period of time. I learned the inner workings of program review, program development, assessment of student learning, general education, human resources, financial aid, marketing, fundraising, grants, budget, strategic planning, academic advising, admissions, developmental education, student retention, facilities, and countless other dimensions of how colleges work—all because everyone *needed* data. I also learned, however, that not everyone *wanted* data.

This reality was underscored by a memorable interaction that occurred when I delivered a presentation on student learning assessment at an all-faculty meeting. A senior faculty member opened the discussion by shouting, "I don't see the need for all this assessment stuff. I'm an economist and I've learned there are three types of lies in this world—lies, damn lies, and statistics! All this assessment and these statistics can only be used for no good." Although community colleges have come a long way in working with data over the past twenty-five years, those sentiments from more than two decades ago still live today on our campuses.

The current challenge has evolved from everyone needing data to everyone needing insights from the data. Information is so readily available that institutions can quickly be overwhelmed and lost in a sea of information. In recent years, many leaders have sought to build within their institutions a culture of evidence wherein data are infused in units throughout the organization. While a culture of evidence is important, a significant corollary is the element of curiosity, which cannot be overlooked. The key is to foster a contagion of curiosity that allows an organization to ask probing questions and pursue data that will yield the most meaningful insights. To ask probing questions, an organization must develop a culture of inquiry.

Fundamental principles fostering a culture of inquiry include:

- *Safety*—Leaders and staff need to trust data and the manner in which it will be used without fear of retribution.
- *Rationale*—The application of data in decision-making is far from intuitive within college cultures; a case must continually be made to faculty and staff of the need for fundamental change in long-standing behavior.
- *Systems Thinking*—Data is connected to every aspect of organizational behavior; a culture of inquiry promotes systems thinking with attention paid to the interconnectedness of data throughout the enterprise.
- *Infrastructure*—Resources must be provided to ensure that colleges can develop and sustain the necessary access to data and analysis that enhance the decision-making process.
- *Focus*—Efforts must be made to identify an overarching framework for the organization to recognize the importance of data and analysis in setting goals, determining interventions for change, and assessing results.
- *Planning*—Strategic, annual, and departmental planning should work differently in a culture of inquiry with traditional wordsmithing giving way to meaningful dialogue about objectives, success metrics, and data definitions and analysis that are easily understood.
- *Performance*—Competing on culture requires attention to performance— not just measuring performance, but with a focus on continuous improvement throughout the organization.
- *Analytics*—A critical challenge in a culture of inquiry is asking questions that get to the root cause of problems through leading indicators that prompt proactive intervention in contrast to reactive measures leading to marginal and unclear results.
- *Inquiry*—Finding ways to encourage and cultivate a sense of curiosity and inquiry is an essential step in transforming culture. Questioning, observing, and pursuing constant improvement counters the natural tendency of organizations toward inertia.

SETTING THE STAGE

Community colleges are facing the challenges associated with fundamental change. The student completion agenda dominating the national narrative highlights the importance of graduation rates while most community college budgets are still driven by enrollment. Graduation and enrollment goals create conflicting agendas within colleges. Among many examples of this conflicted reality is the example of how enrollment gains that come from students registering after the first day of classes have negative consequences in the form of elevated failure rates among late registrants.

Probing areas of organizational performance that make leaders and staff uncomfortable comes with a price. When employees become anxious or fearful, they shut down, personal defenses go up, and communication becomes strained. Fear can take flight in simply not knowing why events are happening or what changes may be looming. Given the transformative implications of suddenly "knowing" what was previously unknown, care must be taken to set the stage for change and draw employees out of darkness and toward light.

Making It Safe

In the same way that trust is a key ingredient of a vibrant organizational culture, trust is at the heart of fostering a culture of inquiry. In *Joy, Inc.*, Richard Sheridan, CEO of Menlo Innovations, wrote, "We pump fear out of the room, filter out ambiguity and anxiety, adjust the cultural temperature to the setting that makes the team comfortable, and then pump safety back in."[1] It's important to create conditions where people feel safe, not a place where people are *striving* to feel safe—make it safe.

Certainly a key principle in infusing data throughout an organization is a clear statement of the intent of using data for improvement, not punishment. Because data is open to interpretation, and even perceived as false by some on campus, staff can become data averse. If there are signals of negative consequences or retribution for asking questions, a desired level of trust is not in place for staff to believe that data will be used solely for the purpose of improvement.

Unfortunately, the academic environment in many colleges does not support transformation to a culture of inquiry because debate is confused with interpretation. Debating opinion is not the same thing as interpreting the meaning and implications of data. Although productive debate is a hallmark of a healthy culture, misplaced debate has consumed countless hours of faculty and administrative time while undercutting efforts to move data to the fore in decision-making. For culture to nurture widespread inquiry, thoughtful questions and informed debate need to be encouraged in ways that recognize and reward the use of data.

Making the Case for Data

Having transitioned in my career into new and different cultures at the level of director, vice president, and president, my experience with culture is similar to what colleagues have described as part of their own career journey. Many cultures are full of *white noise*: ancillary arguments and concerns that are several layers removed from core issues regarding student success, community connections, strategic positioning of the college for the future, and overall employee well-being.

Cultures ooze with distracting debates about employee matters that give voice to the concerns of a small minority that talks over a silent majority and overshadows mission-critical issues. I remember the occasion on which a new president visited a class I had in graduate school. Along with my fellow students, I was eager to learn about the issues a new president might face when taking the reins of an organization as complex as a community college. When asked about the most pressing issue when she arrived on campus, she replied, "The most pressing issue when I arrived on campus was to do something about the goose poop that was covering the sidewalks by the pond at the entrance to our main building."

Exhausting debates can be witnessed and experienced at campus governance meetings on subjects such as changing the academic calendar, synchronizing clocks on campus, smoking on campus, and issues that should only be worthy of debate when graduation rates rise to 75 percent or more or employee and student satisfaction rates are above 95 percent on all criteria. When critical issues are sidelined to make way for personal agendas, organizational culture is held hostage.

Processes and systems can be easily compromised by poor design or data voids and by disengaged employees laboring to hijack visible progress. A challenge many leaders face is one of minimizing "white noise" by redirecting energy toward meaningful dialogue informed by data. Models and strategies employed by organizations outside of education can be helpful in developing an understanding of how analytics and inquiry can be used to shape culture. Data analytics have transformed organizations in retail, advertising, healthcare, and banking. Advances in technology and digitization combined with economic pressure are key factors encouraging industries to use data and analytics to forge business insights and improved decision-making."[2]

Keys to success include:

- Start with high-value questions and a strategy and purpose for data analysis.

- The smallest edge makes the biggest difference when attention is paid to small-scale, connected analyses.
- Insights live at the boundaries between data sets and can be tapped if findings are linked link to complete a big picture for improved problem-solving.
- Loops beat lines because analytics involve more trial and error than straight linear solutions.
- Design matters to participants who need easily accessible tools to conduct the important work of analytics and interpretation.
- Analytics is important, but adoption is the critical step that makes the difference between success and failure.
- Analytics is a team sport that requires multidisciplinary teams with varied expertise to cover all angles of analysis.[3]

These keys can be used to develop elements of a culture of inquiry in which colleges move from a milieu in which the loudest opinionated voice wins, to a place where the most productive interpretation of data wins. The Scottish writer Andrew Lang is credited, in a speech about politicians, with the statement, "Politicians use statistics as a drunken man uses lamp posts— for support rather than for illumination."[4]

The same can be said for administrators, faculty, and staff on any campus. The names and faces may change, but the arguments are remarkably similar. Leaders are continually exposed to vacuous arguments. A particularly acute instance occurred when a dean of communication reported to me that he made some progress on changing the placement test process for developmental English. John had shared some recent placement data at an English Department meeting and a senior faculty member took exception to it.

The faculty member said, "Bob, I've told you this for years now—there's no reason to change what we're doing, the students just aren't prepared!" The dean was able to gain some traction when he pointed out that "Bob" was the dean . . . two deans ago. John affirmed that the faculty member likely had made this argument to "Bob" in the past, but "John" was here now and the data told a different story. He was then able to dismiss the empty argument and engage faculty in analyzing the data and moving to a more informed conversation to address gaps in the curriculum.

Using data to alter the tone and substance of conversation is important, but just as important is establishing a threshold for staff to believe that data will be used for continuous improvement. Helping staff work through the natural fear of change and instinctive need to hold on to the past is slow and tedious work. Relentless effort is needed to put data sets and easily accessible analysis in front of different groups to spark informed dialogue and develop solutions that address pressing problems facing institutions—debating facts, not opinions.

A great place to start is with leveraging the core values of the organization. Core values are central to culture, and it logically follows that they are foundational elements of inquiry. Many colleges—perhaps most—borrow from one another and build core values on buzzwords: excellence, integrity, change, innovation, results, learning, teamwork, exceeding expectations, unmatched service, continuous improvement, accountability, or an assortment of overused words in academe. Bringing core values to life in the operation of an organization requires inquiry and effective use of data—a connection that needs to be made for staff.

Making the case for data, another approach that plays off core values is a call to excellence. Data rarely reflect "good enough," let alone perfection, so leaders have room to call for more: "Are we satisfied with mediocrity?" Jim Collins in *Good to Great* acknowledges that "good is the enemy of great."[5] Too often, "good" organizations that have and use data rest on their laurels. Results are "good enough" and lull the organization into satisfaction and abandonment—at least temporarily—of the pursuit of new ways of doing things as part of an unrelenting effort to improve. Additionally, Collins found that in organizations built to last, cultures were hardwired with the belief that "good enough never is good enough."[6] The constant push and drive for improvement through questioning and purposeful inquiry is ingrained in these organizations.

The accountability movement is another lever that can be used to support and reinforce a culture of inquiry. Rather than simply reacting to external mandates and adverse publicity surrounding retention, graduation, and job-placement rates, community colleges can reframe the argument by becoming proactive in the use of data. The more an organization uses data, the greater the efficacy becomes with using it. Consequently, the more adept an organization becomes at using data, the more effectively it can interpret data and gain control of the public-domain narrative about key performance metrics. Leveraging these three approaches—use, efficacy, and interpretation—can serve an institution by creating a framework for dialogue and making the case for data throughout the organization.

SUPPORTING THE EFFORT

Creating a culture of inquiry requires groundwork that helps people think differently about information and tethers them to the journey. If data collection and analysis become "one more thing" the effort will be short-lived.

Developing Systems Thinking

Data opens conversations that help employees connect actions with results. A supervisor lecturing an employee about behavioral change in the absence of a solid rationale for doing so is not likely to produce much in the way of noticeable improvement. However, using data to show how individual behavior and action are connected to the larger system can help faculty and staff connect the dots and see their behaviors in new ways. "When people in organizations focus only on their position, they have little sense of responsibility for the results produced when all positions interact. . . . [I]t's difficult to know why something went wrong, just assumed someone-somewhere screwed up."[7]

Developing a systems-thinking approach throughout an organization is critical to increasing capacity for inquiry and analysis. When staff can see connections and patterns versus isolated data points or events, insights surface that feed innovation and problem-solving.

The biggest challenge to any form of change is current practice, which is why feedback is so important. However, feedback cannot be provided in isolation; it must be connected to a larger whole.

Fortifying the Infrastructure

Once employees become comfortable with the intended uses of data and the case for data has been sufficiently made, leaders can reallocate resources toward strengthening infrastructure to support a culture of inquiry. Despite the insightful advice my doctoral advisor gave me twenty-five years ago, many community colleges continue to struggle with their institutional research (IR) function, let alone embark on a path of building a culture of inquiry. With accountability mandates accelerating, IR staff are stretched to simply keep up with required reporting—particularly at smaller institutions. And worse yet, many IR professionals labor in isolation, longing to provide middle and senior management with useful information—but too often find little interest or capacity to receive it.

Years ago, the focus of IR was on enrollment analysis, student profiles, surveys, program review, and ad hoc requests. Today, the function has expanded to include sophisticated enrollment analysis and projections, voluminous surveys, cohort tracking, complex developmental education analyses, student and employer focus groups, cost efficiency analysis, graduate follow-up research, and ad hoc requests that are more frequent and complex. Additionally, the increase in grant activity at most colleges has added a new layer of activity and complexity to the IR function, making it a commonly undervalued, underresourced, and underutilized part of the overall operation.

Compounding this challenge is the fact that highly qualified IR staff are hard to find. The Association of Institutional Research indicates that only fifteen universities offer graduate certificates in institutional research.[8] This means that the majority of IR professionals are likely coming to the role requiring a fair amount of on-the-job training. Getting data to the masses can present a substantial challenge for a professional learning on the job in a high-demand, high-stress environment.

Information technology (IT) is an important infrastructure component that can help address gaps in the IR function. If finding and hiring qualified IR staff is problematic, investing in technology can be useful. Unfortunately, internal resistance can inhibit progress for institutional priorities like data accessibility. An unproductive dynamic that regularly occurs on many campuses is the angst of IR professionals needing access to data elements in the information management system, using specialized software, or competing for access and support while the IT department struggles with meeting intensifying demands, maintaining the integrity of information systems, and providing necessary support. By using secondary report tools like Argos or other report writers, standard, canned reports can replace ad hoc requests with timely solutions in the hands of end users and add capacity to the IR function.

A culture of inquiry will encourage widespread data use on campus. As Swing and Ewing-Ross stated, "IR has left the office."[9] As a result, some colleges have turned to sophisticated dashboards that provide web access to charts, graphs, and tables with a few mouse clicks. Data dashboards and data warehouses are useful if data elements are fully developed through user-centered design and the staffing to support it—otherwise, they can be nothing more than an expensive shiny toy for senior administrators.

A culture of inquiry requires a robust infrastructure that can produce clean and reliable data. The requirement for clean data requires IR staff to work in tandem with all departments that enter and use data. Admissions, registrar, financial aid, advisors, academic affairs, and the business office need to be aware of the importance of data entry and trained in the implications their work has on downstream data analysis. Unfortunately, these departments have unique subcultures, priorities, and processes that need to mesh if the data infrastructure of a college is to include data that is consistent and clean throughout operations.

A default model of data infrastructure would consist of a robust IR function supported by an IT department with users throughout the college accessing reliable data. But as stated earlier, analytics is a team sport. A culture of inquiry requires an infrastructure and governance system that supports data use and analysis. Councils, committees, workgroups, and department teams comprised of individuals engaged in purposeful conversation informed by relevant data is the threshold upon which creativity and solutions come into play.

Consider the work of institutional effectiveness councils, student success committees, developmental education task forces, enrollment management workgroups, and specialized teams all operating simultaneously within a college. All need access to data and administrative support to understand and interpret data. In interchange about what data mean and development of recommendations to resolve issues surfaced by data, the organization needs to be clear on the purpose, role, and scope of data user groups: how they are to engage stakeholders in the dialogue; how they relate to governance entities; and how recommendations should flow through the governance system of the college.

Governance is often an overlooked component of the infrastructure required to support a culture of inquiry. Leaders should pay careful attention to the flow of data through the governance system and the impact of data on decision-making. With more intentionality, leaders can use data to prompt, guide, and shape college-wide conversations to increase engagement and understanding among faculty and staff.

CREATING FOCUS

When clearly stated goals are combined with consistent measurement indices and aligned behavior, results are realized. Individuals are motivated and begin to understand the importance and power of the behavior they are being asked to model. Momentum builds as positive behavior generates results and early success provides the foundation for long-term success. [10]

Venturing into data without direction can be a fool's errand and create negative organizational energy. If data are simply presented without context or purpose, they can easily be dismissed and explained away. "People in organizations are extraordinarily talented at normalizing deviant events, at reconciling outliers to a central tendency, at producing typifications, at making do with scraps of information, and at treating as sufficient whatever is at hand."[11] This organizational dysfunction can be addressed by creating a culture of inquiry and a galvanizing framework for culture.

Achieving the Dream as Framework

Although it may not fit for every community college, one approach to creating an overarching framework for inquiry is to participate in the Achieving the Dream Network (ATD). As illustrated by the case studies in chapter 2, participation in ATD can serve as an important catalyst toward creating a culture of inquiry. Some critics still point to earlier research studies that highlighted the failure of some early ATD colleges to make substantial gains on stated goals and student success.[12]

Those criticisms, however, are cast through the narrow lens of short-term impact and fail to account for organizational readiness and capacity to pursue fundamental reform as called for by membership in ATD. If the culture of a college is not positioned to accept the transparency, critical conversations, and organizational reflection called for by ATD to close achievement gaps that have endured for decades, the likelihood of success will be marginal. Referencing Peter Drucker's famous quote about strategy and culture, ATD may provide wonderful strategies to improve student success, but if the culture is not ready, it will eat those strategies for breakfast.

It can be overwhelming to put in place everything that needs to be in alignment to benefit from membership in ATD. A college needs stable, visionary, engaged, and positive leadership—this at a time when many boards experience perpetual turnover and presidential tenure is less than five years. Trust must be evident in a critical mass of staff who believe that ATD participation is genuine, that data will actually be used—for the right reasons—and that transformation will not be confused with just another fad. Organizational support must be available and evident to encourage staff to give up normative behavior and make room for the significant effort ATD requires. And a college must have made progress toward a culture of inquiry with data being collected and used throughout the college. Anything short of all-out effort will leave a college at the foot of a mountain looking at a summit that is clearly out of reach.

For colleges with an adequate level of organizational readiness, ATD or a similar resource can be an accelerator that provides leverage toward the development of an inquisitive culture. No other community college reform effort to date has had such a broad reach as ATD. With more than 220 member community colleges committed to enhancing student success and sharing insights, models, and best practices, ATD is a powerful resource for colleges in a position to put its capabilities to good use.

ATD colleges are provided with a leadership coach and a data coach. These coaches can add significant value for colleges, as they help leadership teams and organizational units sort out issues and create solutions to roadblocks that arise when working through ATD processes. Regular visits to campus enable coaches to provide cadence and rhythm to work and elevate the level of accountability exercised by workgroups in updates and report outs during visits.

The ATD capacity framework includes seven critical capabilities.[13] I have added personal adjectives to the list of ATD capabilities to capture how they should be described when brought to life in a campus culture.

1. Leadership and Vision—steady and inspiring
2. Data and Technology—reliable and robust
3. Equity—inclusive and courageous
4. Teaching and Learning—engaging and adaptive
5. Engagement and Communication—active and meaningful
6. Strategy and Planning—aligned and measurable
7. Policies and Practices—student-focused and evolving

While this framework captures the essential elements of cultural transformation, the data and technology capacity is central to advancing the entire framework. Working with data and getting the right application of technology to support data analysis is a challenging process.

One method many ATD colleges have used to open dialogue around the seven capacities is the data summit. As a college-wide event centered on data, a data summit can be a significant lever for changing the conversation in a college. Faculty and staff operate with assumptions that carry them through the day. Leaders making isolated statements like "We need to improve our graduation rate" pales in comparison to the impact of a half- or full-day work session for the entire college.

Boldly displaying actual retention and graduation rates for all to see grabs the attention of everyone in the room. Pushing matters a step further and breaking data down by subgroup with overall rates, followed by gender, race, ethnicity, age, income level, and other factors is an eye-opening experience. Providing an opportunity for faculty and staff to review and discuss data in small groups raises individual and collective awareness about student success throughout a college. Consequently, conversations move from being shaped by disparate levels of engagement and uninformed assumptions to active attention coupled with informed concern.

Sharing data through a data summit experience or other college-wide event helps to democratize data. It moves data out from the fugitive shadow of isolated departments and committees and allows for broad dialogue and sharing of perspective. Staff have greater access to data and share a common experience that demonstrates how data can be used at a college. Opening up data into the larger organizational culture sets the stage for strategic applications of data that can change the future course of the institution.

4DX as Catalyst

Another approach that colleges are using to transform culture is the Four Disciplines of Execution (4DX) from the Franklin-Covey organization. The Alamo Community College District in San Antonio, Texas, instituted a district-wide "wildly important goal" (WIG) to increase the number of graduates from 6,300 to 7,000 (11 percent) in eighteen months. With full implementation of 4DX, they increased the number of graduates by 18 percent in eight months.[14]

4DX involves a simple framework requiring diligence and focus to implement. The first discipline of execution is to focus on wildly important goals (WIGs). When Alamo set their WIG to increase student completion, they created two hundred teams across the district's five colleges to set smaller WIGs that aligned with the overarching WIG. Teams set no more than two small WIGs to maintain focus on the overarching WIG and make the other disciplines doable. The second discipline calls for colleges to act on lead measures that predict lag measures. A lag measure, like graduation rates, provides results after the fact that inhibit action.

In contrast, a leading measure like retention is a result that can inform graduation rates. To move one step further, course completion can be a leading measure of retention. Lead measures are all about using data for action more than reflection. Maintaining a scorecard is essential to engagement so that everyone knows if a team is winning and advancing lead and lag measures. When teams create their own scorecard they are more likely to maintain focus on achieving a goal.

Finally, creating a cadence of accountability through a weekly 20–30-minute team meeting for group members to report on activities and commitments toward the WIG over the past week is a helpful step in goal achievement. All members review the status of lead and lag measures and stay connected to the overall WIG on a regular basis. To say this kind of accountability is uncommon in community colleges is an understatement. The four disciplines provide a simple and useful framework for transformation to a culture of engagement and inquiry.[15]

Rethinking Strategic Planning

Hardwiring data and continuous improvement into strategic planning can transform how an institution approaches the future. Community colleges run the spectrum of planning infrastructure from smaller colleges having no dedicated staffing to larger colleges with robust planning offices. Regardless, most all colleges have adopted the standard process of conducting an external scan—of varying depth and quality—in tandem with an internal scan followed by gap analysis to identify strategic goals and action steps. This front-end process typically results in lofty written goals with enough wiggle room for administrators to weave in unanticipated initiatives that emerge over the course of the planning period.

In a best-case scenario, a college will have a parallel set of institutional effectiveness indicators that measure progress on key performance indicators (KPI). KPIs are generally only seen by the board of trustees and the cabinet/leadership team. If they are shared throughout the college community, it is generally a surface effort that fails to drive data deep into the culture.

At the far end of the spectrum are community colleges operating in the stratosphere with planning. Namely, colleges that have developed an infrastructure of grids, graphics, and charts outlining how goals, initiatives, and action plans line up with timelines, roles, and responsibilities. Such comprehensive systems may serve the senior leadership well, but defy the understanding of employees who are quickly mired in the complexity of tracking tools and information. A culture of inquiry can create a planning process taking the best from each of these models. Strategic planning in a culture of inquiry tightens the narrative of strategic goals by integrating KPIs with the goals and allows for flexibility through robust departmental planning that advances the strategic plan.

Planning from the Outside, In

The external scan component of strategic planning varies greatly across colleges. It can range from a meeting of program advisory committee members providing input to an academic department or a committee reviewing census and labor statistics and projections to broad-based community and stakeholder focus groups. As described in the case studies in chapter 2, cultural transformation requires planning processes that enable an outside voice to be heard. A culture of inquiry will not develop in an insular culture having conversations with itself. Leaders need to open the planning environment to create space for additional perspectives.

This can be accomplished by identifying major stakeholders in the community, convening profile groups of students, and engaging faculty and staff in a conversation about the future of the college. Modifying the Lorain County Community College Vision 2.0 planning model, Mohawk Valley Community College developed an interview protocol in conjunction with local consultants who provided training to the president's cabinet and selected faculty and staff on focus group facilitation with community organizations. Focus groups engaging representatives from more than one hundred organizations in every sector of the service region were a powerful and uplifting experience.

Combined with focus groups and surveys of faculty, staff, and students, a total of 874 individuals participated in the assessment. The result coming out of a four-month process was a report with insights and themes that provided the Strategic Planning Council with a perspective to combine conversational data with quantitative data on population, job growth, and enrollment projections, as well as institutional effectiveness data embedded in our KPIs.

Metrics versus Narrative

An important event in the progression of Mohawk Valley toward a culture of inquiry was a decision by the Strategic Planning Council to "put some stakes in the ground" in our second year of participation in Achieving the Dream. This move was driven by student success data as part of our ATD work and the leveraging effect of clear objectives. Establishing defined targets for performance rerouted strategic planning at MVCC. We replaced our previous strategic priorities like "student success" and "academic excellence," with action-oriented strategic goals like "Increase student success," and "Strengthen the educational pipeline." (See appendix D.)

Descriptive initiatives in the old plan like "Enhance the student intake system" and "Refine systems that support underprepared students" were replaced with quantitative objectives like "Increase the three-year graduation rate by 20 percent (from 23 percent to 28 percent)" and "Increase the number of partners offering bachelor and graduate programs on campus to five and students enrolled in bachelor's and master's programs at the College by 200 percent."

Shifting from narrative-based priorities and initiatives to metric-based goals and objectives produced some unexpected results that in retrospect seem obvious. The Strategic Planning Council spared itself the mind-numbing task of collectively wordsmithing verbs and adjectives that are part of a narrative-based approach. In a metric-based approach, leaders and staff must be comfortable working with data.

When a subgroup proposed increasing the graduation rate by 30 percent, someone asked, "Why 30 percent? The graduation rate hasn't moved plus or minus 1 percent in the last ten years, what makes us think it will move now?" That question launched a monthlong process to determine the difference between conservative, realistic, and aspirational objectives. We engaged the Board of Trustees in the conversation and, after some deliberation, reached agreement to pursue aggressively realistic objectives.

Although the group process of setting tangible objectives was similar to wordsmithing, the dialogue seemed far more meaningful—and challenging. When the Strategic Planning Council reached agreement on the very first objective under the goal to increase student success and increase the three-year graduation rate by 20 percent, everyone was excited about how good it felt to have such clarity.

We put what felt like an aggressively realistic stake in the ground with a 20 percent increase only to have the Director of Institutional Research and Analysis ask, "How would you like me to define that? More specifically, which of the six different ways I report that statistic would you like me to use—the definition for IPEDS, ATD, VFA, National Benchmarking Project, New York State Department of Education, or the State University of New York? They all use different cohort definitions." The work was different and challenging, but we reached consensus on clear definitions for all objectives.

Annual Plan Development

In the past, the Strategic Planning Council would set forth college-wide initiatives to guide departmental planning at MVCC. Too often, however, faculty and staff would struggle to see themselves and their individual plans and goals reflected in the college plan. With our strategic plan focused on five broad goals to advance thirteen specific objectives over the next five years, the initiatives and action items readily came forward through the departmental plans.

This greatly strengthened a departmental planning process that had been a budget-focused exercise in years past. In the new system, departments could more easily develop their own annual plans to map out their part in advancing metric-based objectives (e.g., how will the Registrar's Office contribute to increasing the graduation rate by 20 percent?).

Peter Drucker is credited with coining the phrase "What gets measured gets managed." By adding clarity to what needs to get measured, the entire college community became acutely aware of what is important. We still have miles to go, but reframing the strategic plan from a narrative-based plan to a metric-based plan with clear objectives and carefully crafted definitions for each metric was a catalyst toward advancing a culture of inquiry and helped change the tenor of key conversations in the college.

FORGING LINES OF INQUIRY

"If you do not know how to ask the right question, you discover nothing."[16] This quote from W. Edward Deming perfectly represents a major stumbling block for colleges struggling to create a culture of inquiry. While modern technologies have made data analysis incredibly precise, the actual experience of working with data can be messy and convoluted. Organizations can lose energy and interest in working with data after experiencing false starts and dead-end paths of inquiry that are commonplace in this work. The path to the right question is rarely straight or easily visible. Most often it is full of starts and stops that challenge even the hardiest of practitioners.

I remember interviewing for the position of Director of Institutional Research and Planning many years ago when I was asked, "What kind of reports would you run to illustrate student retention?" This was a first-generation job in a brand-new IR Office. Rather than responding with what I thought the committee wanted to hear with t-tests, regressions, or some other statistical analysis, I responded that, "I would run frequencies and percentages by demographic group. I've found that dialogue is the most important thing and you can get that started more readily with frequencies and percentages." It was not because of that single answer, but I got the job and found success in providing clear and accessible data using that same philosophy.

Sometimes the most useful questions are found through unassuming lines of inquiry. When graduation rates have failed to move up or down for a decade or more at some colleges, a decision to elevate key metrics like graduation can be painfully easy. One year prior to joining the Achieving the Dream Network, MVCC hosted Jim Simpson and asked him to share key action steps to increase graduation rates. He suggested starting with a review of policies and procedures to identify barriers to student completion.

Our internal policy for late registration was our first barrier. At the time, 76 percent of MVCC students who registered for a class after the first day did not successfully complete the class. This population represented 80 FTE (full-time equivalent) enrollment in the midst of already declining trends, but discontinuing late registration was the right thing to do. Eliminating a graduation fee, which represented yet another barrier, was also a simple step. We replaced it with a lower student support fee charged to all students that also paid for Gallup StrengthsFinder codes that all of our students take in a required College Success Seminar in their first semester.

We were not in a position to automate processes as Jim Simpson suggested, but our Registrar's Office began running degree audits for students with more than sixty credit hours and found more than two hundred *currently enrolled* students had *already met graduation requirements* for a certificate or degree. Students were notified and invited to walk at the next graduation ceremony.

As we got more comfortable working with data and joined the Achieving the Dream Network, our first data summit demonstrated the value of sharing data with all employees. Many were shocked to learn that our three-year graduation rate was 23 percent and had not moved more than 1 percent either way for more than a decade. Worse yet, we needed to own significant achievement gap for Hispanic and African American students graduating at rates far lower than the institutional average.

At our annual data summit three years later, I had the opportunity to review twenty-two action steps taken in the intervening years to increase low graduation rates. It was a special moment when I shared progress data that showed graduation rates move from 23 percent to 31 percent overall; from 14 percent to 26 percent for Hispanics and 8 percent to 18 percent for African American students.

Momentum builds and conversations change when leaders and staff grow comfortable with data. A framework like the one championed by Achieving the Dream gets people thinking and talking about the impact of scaling. Taking inspiration and motivation from the notion of scale within gateway courses subsequently prompted us to make this construct the centerpiece of a successful Title III grant. Gateway courses are the highest-enrolled courses with the lowest student success rates. To increase our student success rate, it made sense to start with these courses. It is a wonder sometimes that community colleges are more than a century old and these conversations are less than a decade old on most campuses.

Importance of Analytics

Data analytics are making a major impact on several industries. From health-care and banking to insurance, manufacturing, and retail, gains are being made in quality, service, and production. Ironically, postsecondary institutions that prepare the workforce for this quickly evolving field are just starting to scratch the surface with applying analytics to their own operations.

As competition intensifies, community colleges that understand and use data will emerge as winners in the future. Colleges can use analytics as leverage to make better and more efficient decisions on key performance indicators. Understanding analytics is a critical first step. The Davenport/Harris Framework captures the central elements of analytics. [17]

These questions simplify analytics into a useful framework throughout the organization. Whether it be faculty reviewing student learning data, administrators reviewing KPIs, or frontline staff reviewing student satisfaction data, these questions guide analysis and dialogue that are critical to fostering a culture of inquiry. I wish I had had this framework twenty years ago when thinking about student completion and our traditional measures were fall-to-fall retention and graduation rates. Analytics go beyond the "what" and get to the "why" of data.

Rob Johnstone calls these traditional lagging indicators "oh crap" measures—because we look at these lagging indicators about what has already happened and say, "Oh crap, it's too late to do anything about that cohort of students." [18] Spending more time on leading indicators provides insights on data that can drive decisions before it is too late. For example, fall-to-fall retention is not a very good measure of student progress. Rather, tracking how many students completed fifteen or more credit hours in their first semester and have thirty or more credit hours are far better leading indicators for the extent to which students are on track for graduation.

	Types of Reporting	Focus
Analytics	Optimization	What's the best that can happen?
	Predictive Modeling	What will happen next?
	Forecasting/Extrapolation	What if these trends continue?
Queries	Statistical Analysis	Why is this happening?
	Alerts (Real Time)	What actions are needed?
	Query/Drill Down (Real Time)	Where exactly is the problem?
	Ad Hoc Reports (Real Time)	How many, how often, where?

Figure 5.1. Data Analytics Framework. T. H. Davenport and J. G. Harris (2007), *Competing on Analytics.*

Like several other service industries, higher education needs to build capacity and accelerate efforts to support analytics—predictive analytics in particular. Community colleges can model what is already being seen in service industries like healthcare. Patients' medical records are entered into sophisticated software systems that track and analyze their health information and provide medical providers with useful data to predict what type of care and health services will be needed. Similarly, how might colleges leverage tools like Starfish, Civitas, and others that claim to have the ability to provide predictive analytics for students? Colleges are already prototyping new models of student support that leverage well-designed data collection and enhanced systems that can act on the personalized information.

Picture a new student going through a standard admissions and registration process with multiple touch points in admissions, advising, registration, financial aid, and the business office to send them on their way for the fall semester only to drop out due to "life issues." Imagine that same student at a college that collects "life issues" prior to registering for classes in the first semester. The student discloses that they are experiencing food and housing insecurities; are mired in legal issues and financial hardship in a divorce and custody battle; is underemployed and has a learning disability.

All of that goes into a system that helps connect the student to appropriate supports before the semester even begins and monitors class attendance and assessments throughout the semester, as well as activity like accessing advising, tutoring, library, and other services at the college. Based on these analytics, a personal communication plan can be enacted to engage the student and connect them with necessary ongoing supports throughout the semester. Examples like this will come to define how community colleges transform the student experience in the very near future.

Unfortunately, integrating analytics into the ongoing operation of a college remains a significant challenge for community colleges. Data analysis is typically the domain of Institutional Research or a similar administrative office. Without widespread engagement, analytics will remain an "add-on" activity versus a strategic lever for institutional improvement.

CLOSING THOUGHTS

Change is uncomfortable and, for most of us, our natural tendency is to justify the present. Creating a culture of inquiry sets an organization into constant forward motion—continually seeking insights and adjusting strategy and operations. Transformation requires setting the stage by easing staff into working with data and understanding why and how data will be used. Inquiry inherently questions the status quo and culture naturally defends the status quo. Systems thinking can change this orientation by broadening the lens through which leaders and staff ask questions.

With investment in infrastructure along with an organizing framework to minimize complexity, a broad organizational focus can emerge to transform culture and enhance performance. Finally, weaving metrics into strategic planning and asking the right questions can institutionalize the habit of inquiry and sustain the organization into the future. For it is the college with a culture of evidence and inquiry that will forever be improving and positioning itself for success in a constantly changing and increasingly complex environment.

NOTES

1. Sheridan, R. (2013). *Joy, Inc.* New York. Penguin Group.
2. Garg, A., Grande, D., Macías-Lizaso Miranda, G., Sporleder, C., and Windhagen, E. (2017). "Analytics in Banking: Time to Realize the Value." McKinsey & Company. April, 2017.
3. Ibid.
4. Mackay, A. L. (1977). *The Harvest of a Quiet Eye: A Selection of Scientific Quotations.* Madison, WI: Institute of Physics.
5. Collins, J. (2001). *Good to Great.* New York. HarperCollins.
6. Collins, J. (1994). *Built to Last.* New York. HarperCollins.
7. Senge, Peter M. (1990). *The Fifth Discipline.* New York: Doubleday. 19.
8. "Graduate Certificates in Institutional Research." Association of Institutional Research. https://www.airweb.org/Careers/GraduateEducation/Pages/default.aspx (accessed June 18, 2017).
9. Swing, R. L., and Ewing-Ross, L. (2016). "A New Vision for Institutional Research." *Change.* March/April, 2016, 7.
10. Studer, Q. (2003). *Hardwiring Excellence.* Gulf Breeze, FL: Firestarter Publishing. 63.
11. Weick, K. E., and Daft, R. L. (1983). "The Effectiveness of Interpretation Systems." In *Organizational Effectiveness: A Comparison of Multiple Models.* K. S. Cameron and D. A.Whetten (eds.). New York. Academic Press. 87.
12. Gonzalez, J. (2011). "'Achieving the Dream' Produces Little Change at Community Colleges." *The Chronicle of Higher Education.* February 9, 2011.
13. Achieving the Dream. *Achieving the Dream's Institutional Capacity Framework and Institutional Capacity Assessment Tool.* http://achievingthedream.org/sites/default/files/basic_page/atd_icat_assessment_tool.pdf. Website accessed March 20, 2018.
14. Leslie, B. (2016). *4DX at Alamo Colleges.* Strategic Horizon Colloquium. San Antonio. October 22, 2016.
15. McChesney, C., Covey, S., and Huling, J. (2012). *The Four Disciplines of Execution.* New York. Free Press.
16. The W. Edwards Deming Institute, "Large List of Quotes by W. Edwards Deming." https://blog.deming.org/w-edwards-deming-quotes/large-list-of-quotes-by-w-edwards-deming/
.
17. T. H. Davenport and J. G. Harris (2007), *Competing on Analytics: The New Science of Winning*, Boston: Harvard Business School Press.
18. Johnstone, R. (2017). *Guided Pathways Demystified.* Presentation to Mohawk Valley Community College. September 21, 2017.

Chapter Six

Tomorrow

A Culture of Anticipation

What we need to do is always lean into the future; when the world changes around you and when it changes against you—what used to be a tail wind is now a head wind—you have to lean into that and figure out what to do because complaining isn't a strategy.

—Jeff Bezos, CEO, Amazon [1]

Some colleges survive in spite of themselves. Whether it be cancerous boards, transactional leadership, caustic cultures, insular programs and services, poor student success rates or a combination of variables, community colleges today have weathered a number of shortcomings. The future is not likely to be so kind. Increasingly constrained resources, acute student needs, intensifying accountability demands, and significant societal and technological changes are creating a fast-moving and disruptive environment in which to operate.

Community colleges that thrive in the future will develop mechanisms to better understand the disruptions underway, cultivate an entrepreneurial mind-set through structures and systems that encourage innovation; and create organizational resources that anticipate change rather than reacting to it. By doing so, successful community colleges will likely look different than today and be characterized by a culture of anticipation.

DIGITAL DISRUPTION

Innovation is all about platforms. Like electricity and energy or the automobile and mobility, one innovation can create a cascade of subsequent innova-

127

tions that lead to fundamental transformation. As we transition from the information age to whatever comes next, the importance of platforms is increasingly significant to the acceleration of change. Nanotechnology and sensors are already disrupting our daily lives in subtle ways in everything from personal health to driving to entertainment.

The "Internet of Things" is facilitating changes that would have been considered magic twenty years ago and today are taken for granted in their ubiquitous presence. Similarly, tectonic plates are already in motion for a fundamental disruption in the delivery of educational content as we know it.

Before exploring possibilities in the future of education, a brief examination of the music industry is helpful. Operating in its original form for two short years, Napster was a harbinger of change for the music industry: electronic media music files could be shared via the Internet. As Napster was transitioning through legal battles, Apple launched iTunes in 2001 for use on its computers and its new iPod product. After a series of small-scale improvements, the iTunes Store was launched in 2003 along with a Windows version of iTunes.

With the launch of the iPhone in 2007, the iTunes Store exploded in scale and fundamentally changed the way people access and listen to music. People could buy a single song for 99 cents and conveniently play it on a variety of mobile devices with customizable playlists whenever they wanted. However, within a few short years, streaming music services like Pandora radio became visible forces in a powerful trend toward individualization by allowing listeners to create personalized radio stations that played songs based on listening preferences to suit their musical interests and moods.

More recently, Pandora and other streaming services like Spotify have taken the platform to the next level by offering subscription services that not only provide a wide variety of playlists, but also allow for unlimited access to an ever-expanding inventory of songs that can be organized on customized personal playlists on a variety of Bluetooth-enabled devices. These playlists can then be accessed whenever a listener wants—all of this in fifteen short years from simply sharing a music file on Napster. Who could have thought this would be possible?

A parallel to this music industry metaphor has been evolving right in front of us and is gaining traction. In 1995, the Internet facilitated the development of online educational delivery. Fifteen years later, most community colleges had courses or complete programs offered in online formats, with some engaging 20 percent or more of their student population. While community colleges were using the Internet to grow enrollment, the Massachusetts Institute of Technology was leveraging it to fundamentally rethink access. In 2002, MIT created a website with free content for fifty courses and by 2007 more than 1,800 courses were available cost free.[2]

Open courseware led to the development of massive open online courses (MOOCs). When elite institutions like MIT, Harvard, Stanford, and others launched MOOCs in 2012, news articles were appearing almost daily that created varying levels of panic, dismissal, and wonder among college educators. MOOCs' offering free content from the most well-known universities with scalable design principles enabling tens of thousands of students to enroll in a single course section shook the higher education sector to its core.

Within two years, analyses of dropout rates and problems with alignment of MOOC offerings for credit made it easy for higher education professionals to dismiss MOOCs as a fad that was already passing. In retrospect, however, the early version MOOCs were the Napster of postsecondary education— simply a harbinger of things to come.

As the higher education business model has evolved, online providers are shrinking free content and pursuing more revenue models. Providers like edX, Coursera, and Udacity, the top three MOOC providers, made more than $100 million in 2016.[3] Udacity has increasingly partnered with employers and focused on high-demand workforce needs. Coursera is pursuing a distributed revenue model focused on specializations and microcredentials with content accessible through subscription services, much like the streaming music services. The last remaining nonprofit MOOC of the big three is edX. They have partnered with Arizona State University and others on multiple endeavors such as Global Freshman Academy, which is completely online and cost-free using the edX platform.[4]

Critics labeling the MOOC platform a fad because it overlooks the need for human interaction and connection should not lose sight of the rapid rise of Southern New Hampshire University (SNHU). Competing with online giant University of Phoenix, SNHU has garnered considerable market share in the past few years by providing flexible online programming, comprehensive support services, and high-performance career services with internship and job-placement support for all of its students and alumni.

The digital disruption created by MOOCs and their evolution and the rapid success of Southern New Hampshire University underscore the fact that postsecondary education is costly, time intensive, unscalable, generally impersonal, and mostly inflexible. The wave of the future is a porous educational system where students flow in and out as their learning needs change.[5] This system has the potential to revolutionize education and prompt closures and mergers over the next two decades among institutions that are too insular and slow to adjust. One needs only to look at recent system realignments and mergers in Georgia and Louisiana and proposals under consideration in other states to realize this is possible.

Facing challenges of declining state support and shrinking enrollment, the current postsecondary-education model in this country is unsustainable. If platforms are the key to innovation and MOOCs represent a new delivery platform, what will come next? Insight from the music industry again may help to bring the horizon into view. If MIT's open courseware in 2001 can be viewed as Napster and the original free MOOCs of 2012 as the iTunes Store, the streaming services of Pandora and other high-tech organizations can be considered metaphors for the Global Freshman Academy at Arizona State, the subscription service of Coursera, and employer partnerships with Udacity. Something is afoot in the delivery of postsecondary education that will mirror the intensely personalized and customizable streaming music services of Pandora, Spotify, and others.

MOOCs represent the first time in the past century that community colleges—the original higher education disruptor—risk being truly disrupted themselves. Arguments about the extent to which colleges are facing disruption often trigger "reactions on campuses: either a malaise that the end is near or overconfidence that the good days will return, just as they always have. As a result, institutions rarely introduce the sometimes-radical changes they need to make, because one group of constituents believes the sky will fall tomorrow anyway, while others refuse to acknowledge that this time change is different."[6]

Community college leaders cannot leave the future to chance. Efforts to transform colleges need to be accelerated and new models of educational delivery embraced if our colleges are to remain relevant. Transformation can only be accomplished through cultures that are sufficiently fluid to embrace and advance change.

CHANGING EXPECTATIONS

New models for educational delivery are underway as can be seen in the flipped classroom model popularized by the Khan Academy.[7] With more than three thousand video lectures online, the Khan Academy is used in K–12 school districts and increasingly as a supplement to college courses. The videos replace some or all of the time used for lecture in traditional classrooms and "flip" class time so that the lecture is delivered online at the convenience of the student and "homework" is done on campus in groups and focused time in the classroom, with the instructor serving in the role of "coach" to address individualized learning needs of each student.

I learned firsthand the ease, relevance, and significance of this approach to educational delivery through an experience with our two daughters a few years ago. Our youngest daughter came home from school one day frustrated with her math class. She was feeling discouraged with the teacher's style of straight lecture and spare tolerance for questions. Since her older sister—who was away at college—had the same teacher a few years earlier, she called her for advice.

Her sister asked, "You're sitting in the back of the class, right?"

She replied, "No. I'm sitting in the front trying to pay attention! Why would I sit in the back of the class?"

Her sister said, "You already said she doesn't teach you anything that isn't in the book and doesn't explain it anyway, so you should sit in the back of the class and do your homework."

She replied, "How can I do the homework, when the teacher hasn't taught the lesson?"

Her sister said, "Each night you read the lesson, look at the homework, and then watch the Khan Academy videos on the subject so the next morning you can do your homework in the back of class while the teacher simply bores everybody by regurgitating the textbook."

With increasingly available online resources and tools, kids today have the capacity to flip their own classroom whether faculty want to or not.

This underscores the increasingly significant trend of individualization. From Spotify and the music we play to the predictive analytics of retail marketing with customized ads in our e-mail and on our webpages, individualization will be a defining characteristic of our future.[8] So what does this mean for community colleges? At the core of transformation in educational delivery is rethinking the faculty role. A great lecture is interesting, but even a good lecture falls short when content can be delivered in more engaging and dynamic ways. This reality has become increasingly significant as young learners grow up with access to anything they want to learn, whether it be content they can "Google" or "how to" videos on YouTube. The key will be the extent to which colleges are able to support faculty and staff in redefining roles and responsibilities.

It has yet to be determined how accurate futurist Thomas Frey's prediction of a "teacherless classroom" will be. Frey foresees teachers and trainers being replaced by coaches and mentors.[9] Realistically the answer probably will lie somewhere between what we see today and teacherless experiences for students. As Aaron Weiss, math professor at Lorain County Community College, said, "We are essentially doing missionary work in community colleges, so it's important that we don't take the missionaries out of the equation."[10] The missionaries likely won't leave the mission, they will just likely be working differently with the scripture.

As the unknown future comes into view, Google is increasingly positioning itself to shape educational delivery through the Google Classroom initiative. Google's culture of innovation continues to leverage technology to a position at the front of the educational market.[11] From 2012 to 2017, Google went from providing less than 1 percent of all media devices shipped to public schools to 58 percent.

Google Chromebooks and apps are in more than half of all public school classrooms.[12] Google Classroom puts technology-rich tools and apps in the hands of students that provide teachers with more instructional flexibility. School-age children are having technology-enhanced learning experiences every day from kindergarten through high school—experiences that supersede the typical college classroom experience that remains stuck in low gear. The resulting incongruence will open higher education to further scrutiny and critique and will enable new competitors to enter the marketplace.

In addition to changing expectations of students, community colleges will see expectations of other stakeholders change as well. Employers frustrated with limited talent pools will intensify their demand for qualified graduates with technical and workplace skills as well as essential interpersonal skills. Employers will want customized training for workers designed to meet specific needs.

State and county governments challenged by limited resources and tax caps will demand more and better with less from community colleges on everything from the number of graduates, to economic development and anti-poverty initiatives. Struggling nonprofits and local governments will look to community colleges as anchor institutions to leverage resources to provide capacity and support for community-development activities in ways unseen in the past. Community colleges that cling to the status quo will be overwhelmed and fall into limbo while those that create capacity and anticipate changes will thrive in this new environment.

New Credentials

Associate degrees and certificates have been around for more than a century almost unchanged in their composition of credit hours. Fundamental shifts are underway that mandate new and different forms of credentialing. The landscape of graduate education is changing through the micro-masters offered on the edX platform by universities such as Columbia, the Massachusetts Institute of Technology, the University of Michigan, and others. With free courses available through MOOCs, individuals can work through the content themselves and then pay a modest fee (often less than $3,000) to take the assessment and receive the credential upon successful completion.

Similarly, private vendors experimenting with new models for job training are filling market niches that community colleges have failed to address. For example, the national need for computer programmers is so great that Apple has launched an "Everyone Can Code" initiative to promote and support any and all ways to get more people to code. Computers are so ubiquitous at this point that it would be hard to find a community college without computer applications and/or a computer science degree program. And yet, consider that the need for computer programmers is so great that Apple has made it a significant priority.

Most community colleges are frustrated by the middle-skills gap. According to the National Skills Coalition, 53 percent of all jobs in the United States are classified as middle skill and 48 percent of all job openings require candidates with middle skills. At present, only 43 percent of the current U.S. workforce is qualified with middle skills.[13] Community college educators are discouraged because training and degree programs exist, but enrollments continue to decline despite an abundance of job openings. The root cause is embedded in traditional approaches to educational delivery—offering credit-bearing certificate and degree programs on the normal academic calendar—that simply do not get the job done at the scale employers need.

Coding is a glaring example of how community colleges need to change and change quickly. Fifty years ago, offering evening courses was considered an innovation. Today program delivery is not just about evening, weekend, and online courses, but also about programs and courses that need to be accelerated, compressed, and focused. The Flatiron School in New York City is one of several Coding Bootcamps to emerge on the postsecondary scene in recent years.

With tuition between $5,600 (online) and $12,000 (on campus), Flatiron offers individuals the opportunity to learn computer programming in three to seven months depending on campus or online delivery method. The results are noteworthy: 98 percent placement rate and more than $70,000 starting salary for graduates in their first five years of operation.[14] Clearly, Flatiron is on to something that few colleges could instantly replicate.

Students can complete the boot camps faster than most colleges could get the program approved through a curriculum committee. With cultures bound by tradition, process, and boundaries, most community colleges are not capable of developing and executing something so focused and customer friendly.

In the same way taxi companies were "Ubered" through the disruptive ride-sharing delivery model of Uber, community colleges need to find ways to "Uber" themselves. More than ever, colleges need to reinvent their credit-bearing curriculum (i.e., computer programming or computer science) and repurpose it into boot camp–like formats delivering high-demand/high-yield programming to the community.

Colleges that are unable to "Uber" themselves are missing out on fundamental shifts occurring all around them. Google is disrupting K–12 education, MOOCs are altering graduate education credentials, and boot camps are delivering quality workforce training outcomes faster and more cost-effectively than community colleges. Southern New Hampshire University continues to successfully scale its College for America offerings and online degree programs.

New models for undergraduate education will soon accelerate the pace at which undergraduate education takes alternate forms, very likely with more appeal and better results. And yet, at most community colleges these changes have attracted attention as being "out there," but removed from day-to-day reality where faculty and staff think they have control over what goes on with student learning.

RETHINKING STRUCTURES

Fast-moving competitors require new ways of thinking about how best to compete. Despite increasing pressure from competitors, community colleges are not working with new ideas at a pace that will keep them in front of the educational market. Having adopted fundamental elements of traditional college and university cultures, our colleges are constrained by the current reality of structures, systems, processes, and policies that contribute to inertia in the daily grind.

As Sydow and Alfred state,

> Not surprisingly, perpetually scarce resources and the accretion over time of inefficient systems and practices common to the higher education industry have coalesced to impede the ability of community colleges to establish structures and systems that are conducive to scalable and sustainable innovation. The very characteristics that have enabled our colleges to thrive for more than one hundred years—open access, low cost, convenience, community focus, and responsiveness to local demand—have also positioned them for strategic partnerships and early adoption of new technologies. The problem is that for opportunity and innovation to be successfully pursued, people, organizations, and cultures must be ready for change—a state that currently seems to defy the best efforts of leaders.[15]

Author Steven Johnson argues that innovation comes from open and interconnected environments that provide conditions for creative collisions to occur and produce innovative ideas. Innovation is not a person or team locked in a room for months and years on end trying to come up with the next big thing. It is a culture of openness that allows for the sharing and connecting of ideas that lead to progressively bigger ideas that result in the next big thing.[16]

Community colleges must learn to support and manage "calculated serendipity" by rethinking formal and informal structures that comprise the organization. Understanding innovation is a critical first step toward structuring an environment for creative collisions and accelerating innovation. A helpful way to think about innovation is the following matrix from Satell.[17]

The typical community college is locked in the "Basic Research" box of not-well-defined problems and not-well-defined domains. Reform efforts like Achieving the Dream and Guided Pathways are helping to bring greater clarity that may move colleges to the other boxes. However, innovation is

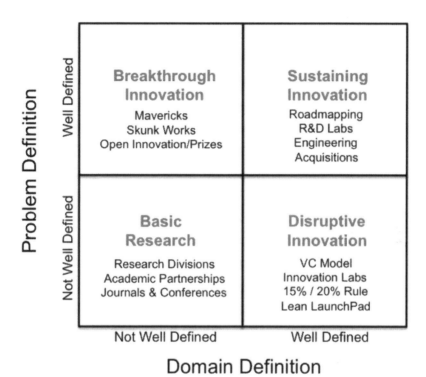

Figure 6.1. Innovation Matrix Satell, G. "4 Types of Innovation and the Problems They Solve."

more likely to take hold when community colleges work to transform culture in meaningful ways through transformational approaches to structure and decision-making.

An often-overlooked dimension of innovation is that clarifying the problem or challenge is equally important to the big idea or novel solution. Leaders need to help cultures clarify more well-defined problems that can lead to breakthrough innovation. Additionally, facilitating a more entrepreneurial culture increases the likelihood for a culture to pursue and embrace disruptive innovation. Through these strategic efforts, leaders can find their colleges moving toward sustaining innovation and thriving where others will simply try to survive.

Organizational structure is the formal component of culture. A compressed organizational chart concentrates power among a few key players, while an expansive structure distributes decision-making power across a broad set of individuals. To create an open environment that increases the likelihood of creative collisions and fosters innovation, community colleges must develop loosely-coupled structures held together through clarity of mission and common understanding of core values.

John Kotter underscores the rational need for hierarchies but goes on to address the limits of such structures. He builds a case for mature organizations to not only manage hierarchies, but also to develop parallel networked structures that operate informally.[18] This rethinking of structure transforms culture from a static, single form to an adaptive hybrid that redefines relationships, roles, and responsibilities, and the overall flow of communication and work itself. Hierarchical and networked structures operating simultaneously in concert with one another is the type of structure that community colleges will need to build in order to compete successfully for the future.

By developing and investing in loosely connected, self-directed teams, college leaders can redistribute power and authority. This redistribution creates flexibility, increases employee engagement, and fosters creativity and innovation as decision-making moves from the center of the organization to peripheral units that are closer to students and stakeholders. Self-managed teams are in the best position to work more closely with internal and external stakeholders and accelerate problem-solving and decision-making.

Menlo Innovations, a software development company in Ann Arbor, Michigan, is completely organized around self-directed teams. With clearly stated organizational values that align with their vision, mission, procedures, and practices, Menlo's self-directed teams operate at a high level of productivity. The company is a seven-time recipient of the Alfred P. Sloan Award for Business Excellence in Workplace Flexibility, but not for the reasons one might normally associate with workplace excellence—flextime, workweek accommodation, or benefits. Menlo's flexibility is all about how their teams operate and the environment in which they work.

Having personally toured the work space (in the basement of a parking garage no less), I have seen firsthand the open environment that has distinct attributes. Signs of positivity abound, from the shared workstations to a simple project-management system. Team members collaborate with clear messages embedded in policies and practices that reinforce values of honoring people over process, providing employees with necessary tools, hiring for and supporting cognitive diversity, and maintaining a focus on the belief that flexibility naturally increases capacity.[19]

MVCC's Executive Director of Information Technology, Paul Katchmar, was intrigued by Menlo's work practices and committed to transforming our IT department into a self-directed work-team structure. By organizing the department into three teams (network, applications, and programming), he was able to redesign department procedures around the new structure. Using the Menlo system of project story cards, team members are now assigned to short-term projects with visible accountability that comes together in team meetings every other Wednesday. These meetings allow team members to learn the status and context of all projects underway in the department. With enhanced transparency, team members are routinely reassigned from project to project depending on what skill sets are needed when.

Through a commitment to inquiry and improvement, Paul and his team have incorporated elements of the Four Disciplines of Execution (4DX) by organizing projects and story cards around departmental "wildly important goals" (WIGs). Lead measures are developed for each project story card and the scoreboard is posted prominently in Paul's office with cards posted on the wall for all to see. The biweekly meeting to review the project story cards creates a cadence of accountability and the Menlo commitment to joy has developed over time to make the signature line for the department, "every other Wednesday we go to work to tell stories and play cards."

After two years of operating with self-directed work teams, the IT department has not only seen a rise in spirit and productivity, but has also recorded striking results in the organizational climate survey. When asked about their satisfaction with various campus departments, employees assigned the highest departmental scores to IT in almost every category. When considering the incredible demands and expectations placed on IT departments these days, an increase in colleague satisfaction with the IT department performance is nothing short of incredible. Their work has garnered the attention of other departments at the college and prompted Paul and a key team member to conduct workshops on self-directed work teams in a number of other departments.

THE CHANGING ROLE OF POWER

Creating a hybrid structure with loosely coupled self-directed teams in a network structure alongside the traditional hierarchy changes power in an organization. The network structure provides avenues to power partly fueled by a younger generation of workers who think and act differently in ways that draw a clear line between "old" and "new" power. Organizational cultures of the future will be greatly influenced by this changing power dynamic.

Old power is like currency in that it belongs to a small closed group of leaders and flows down through narrow organizational channels. New power more closely resembles a current by the way it is open and participatory, with uneven flows, and user driven, as it flows upward and disperses throughout the organization.[20] The participatory attributes of new generations in the workforce are well suited to new power. Unlike the rule-based follower

behavior of old power, new power fosters leadership at all levels by supporting individual creativity with minimal direction while emphasizing connectivity wherever possible to advance organizational strategies.[21] The combination of network structures and new generations bringing different attributes
and interests into the workplace will change power dynamics in organizations and help transform organizational cultures in ways that increase connectivity, innovation, and flexibility.

The Power of Networks

The increasingly complex environment in which community colleges now
operate calls for new approaches to old operations. Traditional approaches
yield traditional solutions that are no longer relevant. Community colleges
need to become networked organizations to succeed in an environment that is
too multifaceted to effectively manage within existing structures.

Colleges that think and act in terms of networks will have staff beyond
the president who are oriented to connecting the college with organizations
in the community. Whether it be faculty elected to school boards, staff in
locally elected positions, or employees in churches and volunteer groups, if
employees are thinking about promoting and connecting the college, the
college will thrive in a virtuous upward spiral of novel and productive link-
ages.

By drawing on social network theory that amplifies the importance of
relationships between network members,[22] community colleges can leverage
common relationships and expand capacity and potential of the whole. Networks go beyond ordinary partnerships that have become so familiar over the
last thirty years and greatly expand efforts to make community colleges more
agile, flexible, and adaptable by incorporating diversity and creativity into
organizational structures and systems.[23]

> *Employer Networks*: By their very nature, community colleges have net-
> works of employers that support internships, serve advisory councils,
> donate equipment and other resources, and hire program graduates.
> Some colleges facilitate or participate in employer consortia, often by
> industry sector. Going forward, community colleges will need to am-
> plify their role as anchor institutions to recast employer partnerships
> and think of them in terms of networks that can address workforce
> needs in new and uncommon ways.
>
> Leveraging networks of employers to scale up modern apprenticeships
> that blend education and work in an updated version of cooperative
> education can increase enrollment in technical programs as well as
> increase job placement rates. Another example of leveraging employer
> networks is through advocacy. Getting networks of employers to help
> tell the community college story to stakeholders such as elected offi-

cials at local, state, and national levels can recast traditional relationships and define new roles through the lens of a network.

Community-Based Organization Networks: Similarly, the anchor institution role for community colleges can galvanize local community-based organizations (CBOs) to form networks to address community challenges. The Bronx Opportunity Network is one such model. City University of New York (CUNY) community colleges Bronx and Hostos have collaborated with seven CBOs to increase college access and success among disconnected youth in the Bronx. Network members have been able to accelerate their efforts by operating as a multi-relational interconnected web of support for youth versus individual—one-to-one—organizational relationships. This networked approach to student success has yielded positive results for participants in the programs offered by the Network.[24]

State and National Networks: Perhaps the most readily accessible networks can be found at the state and national levels. Community colleges in statewide systems such as in Colorado, Florida, North Carolina, Texas, and Virginia have system offices that coordinate statewide initiatives and convene regular statewide meetings. These structures allow for regular interaction and communication that facilitate ideas and innovation. Beyond statewide organizations, national networks like Achieving the Dream and Jobs for the Future Student Success Centers can provide access to best practices and create environments for college teams of faculty and staff to interact with one another. Shared experiences from these activities foster a common vocabulary as well as inspiration and prompts for ideas and innovations to foster within a college culture.

Professional Development Networks: Even more profound than state and national networks are networks created by member institutions themselves. For example, the League of Innovation has been a member-driven organization since 1968 and leveraged the power of networks to promote and support innovation among its members. The network structure of meetings, conferences, and services provides members with access to resources that accelerate organizational development.

Similarly, the Continuous Quality Improvement Network (CQIN) is an organization of more than forty members (nearly all community colleges) that drive their own professional development agenda. With special programs and meetings, CQIN delivers relevant, thought-provoking experiences for participants. Larger CQIN institutes feature corporate partners and learning from disciplines and sectors outside of education that spur innovation and improvement among member colleges.

Consisting of seven like-minded community colleges, the Strategic Horizon Network (SHN) is also a member-driven organization with a more intimate experience. Similar to the League of Innovation and CQIN, SHN is interested in studying disruptive innovation, strategic thinking, and vibrant organizational cultures. Operating in various forms for nearly twenty years, SHN brings teams of faculty and staff from each college together twice a year for dynamic colloquia with programs designed by presidents and an executive liaison from each college.

SHN Program ideas and colloquia content are primarily sought from organizations outside of education with presentations coupled with learning site visits to various organizations:

- agriculture (Rural Council of Vermont)
- banking (Quicken Loans, Bank of New York-Mellon)
- community-based organizations (Pittsburgh Children's Museum, REEL Teens)
- design firms (Menlo Innovations, IDEO).
- food and beverage (Ben & Jerry's, Whole Foods, Zingerman's Deli, the Wine Group)
- healthcare (University of Michigan and St. Joseph Mercy hospitals, Ann Arbor)
- hospitality (Marriott, Keystone Resorts)
- manufacturing (Caterpillar, Honda)
- media (AnnArbor.com)
- professional sports teams (San Antonio Spurs)
- retail (REI)
- technology (Google marketing group, Internet of Things Research Center)

Programs run over the course of two and a half days and provide common learning through uncommon experiences that cannot be found at a typical higher education conference. The design principle of colleges bringing teams of five to ten members amplifies learning with ample opportunity for reflection, conversation, connection, and creativity in applying colloquium content to develop new solutions to contemporary issues. Colleges that participate in peer learning networks like the League, CQIN, or SHN find themselves with rich resources and contacts to accelerate innovation and organizational development.

The resources, opportunities, and experiences brought about by membership in networks infuse positive, forward-thinking behavior into organizational culture. For example, MVCC has taken the SHN Colloquium model and created one-day innovation colloquia using local resources. A recent example included a one-day program for all college administrators focused on the importance of college values in shaping organizational culture. Held at the college's business start-up accelerator, the thINCubator, off-campus in downtown Utica, participants spent the day in a creative learning environment.

Pre-reading assignments of articles had participants walking through the door focused and filled with anticipation. This was not a typical workshop—two local business leaders opened the day, with the first providing a conceptual framework for thinking about culture and the second sharing what his company did to receive the "best place to work" award for companies in New York State with fewer than two hundred employees.

Lunch was served outside from a food truck followed by videos on Zappos' culture, which served as a precursor to interactive table discussions. The group then dispersed into four groups to visit local manufacturers using core values to shape culture and drive change in their organization. Participants reconvened to synthesize and share their experiences before considering applications to the MVCC.

A similar experience for frontline staff was developed around the concept of exceptional experiences. After two morning speakers and lunch, round-table discussions informed by a TED talk on the experience economy were held to consider applications to MVCC. Applications were centered on providing students with a unique experience:

- Treat students like fans: visit the local minor league hockey team.
- Treat students like the star of the show: visit the local Broadway theater venue.
- Treat students like a guest: visit a popular fine dining restaurant.
- Treat students like members: visit the local zoo with exceptional service for members.

Colloquia are being developed in similar fashion with programs on creativity, risk, innovation, and disruption utilizing local employers and speakers—all within the college's local network, at no cost. As resources diminish, community colleges can achieve significant cost benefits by turning to networks to find new capacities that energize faculty and staff.

ENTREPRENEURIAL MIND-SET

Declining public resources combined with rising costs create an environment that requires community colleges to identify and pursue alternative funding streams. Competition for grants will continue to increase, forcing colleges to pursue unconventional funding. For example, establishing a limited liability corporation (LLC) or a social enterprise through an auxiliary corporation or college foundation can create additional revenue above and beyond traditional revenue streams.

Colleges like Tompkins Cortland Community College (TC3) in upstate New York have used hospitality programs as entrepreneurial ventures. TC3 purchased a building in downtown Ithaca and moved its hospitality program off-campus. By establishing the Coltivare bistro as a fully operational restaurant and events center, TC3 established not only a new community asset, but a unique applied-learning environment for students and faculty. As a separate and distinct LLC, Coltivare is an independent operation, but functions as an affiliated organization of the college.[25]

Hospitality is but one of several career-oriented programs with potential for a social enterprise model in community colleges. Other programs such as automotive, welding, graphic design, business, computer science and construction hold great potential for creating social enterprises that employ students, interns, and graduates to meet market needs with profits returning to the college.

An entrepreneurial orientation requires colleges to inventory their assets (e.g., academic programs, land, networks, etc.) and find ways to create revenue-generating solutions. Following the social enterprise model of Ben & Jerry's ice cream with its triple mission of product, economic, and social good, community colleges can use core values to navigate the wide-open landscape of entrepreneurial space.

For example, Montgomery College in Maryland stepped out on its core values of innovation and sustainability to create an entrepreneurial venture by developing a forty-acre parcel of undeveloped land adjacent to its Germantown Campus. Montgomery moved beyond developing a traditional business park to establish an integrated academic, business and research campus with a focus on science and technology working with private sector partner/tenants.

In addition to tech companies, Montgomery partners with county government to provide an incubator for biotech startups, and the county's newest hospital—the first in the country to be located on a community college campus. The college established a new foundation to manage the campus and simultaneously serve as the landlord. Tenants not only provide rent, but also a pool of talented adjunct faculty and accessible applied learning opportunities such as internships and undergraduate research opportunities for Montgomery students.[26]

Morrisville State, an agriculture and technology college within the State University of New York, is one of the more entrepreneurial colleges in the nation with more than 10 percent of its operating revenue coming from ventures in an affiliate 501(c)(3) Auxiliary Services Corporation. Revenue-generating operations include:

- *Horticulture*—full-service flower shop offering sales at farmers markets and online
- *Morrisville Fresh, LLC*—student-run LLC that produces and sells agricultural products
- *Nelson Farms*—separate brand providing entrepreneurial agribusiness opportunities for specialty food processors, farmers, growers, and producers; opportunities include processing/co-packing, product development, dairy incubator, and distribution, marketing and sales
- *Dairy*—fully functional dairy enterprise incorporating the use of a windmill and a methane digester, which offset more than half of electrical expenses
- *Equine*—complex operation to breed, train, rehabilitate, and race horses, and host the largest Standardbred yearling sale in New York State
- *Aquaculture*—operates a controlled environmental agriculture (CEA) system that raises and sells tilapia and rainbow trout
- *Automotive*—operates a full-service automotive repair and body shop open to the public that also repairs and updates donated automobiles for public distribution
- *Massage*—offers massage therapy clinics to the public, college staff and students
- *Travel Agency*—operates a full-service travel agency and partners with Madison County Tourism
- *Restaurant Management*—faculty and students work to operate the full-service Copper Turret restaurant
- *Renewable Energy Training Center*—offers training in solar, wind, geothermal, and micro-hydro energy
- *Environmental Training Center*—offers wastewater operator training for state recertification
- *Renewable Resources*—manages and harvests forested growth from state-owned land
- *Residential Construction*—builds and renovates both on-campus and off-campus projects[27]

Similarly, Central Piedmont Community College in North Carolina created CPCC Services—a separate LLC for the sole benefit of supporting the college. This entrepreneurial enterprise has developed numerous money-making ventures over the past two decades based on ideas brought forward from faculty and staff. From ESL language videos to consulting services, CPCC Services has created an entrepreneurial culture that has nurtured a spirit of innovation throughout the college.

Lorain County Community College (LCCC) in Ohio established a pre-seed fund with a specific focus on supporting entrepreneurs. Through its college foundation, the LCCC Foundation secured more than $20 million in public and private dollars to support economic development and complement its business incubator facility and programs. The fund provides grants of $25,000 and awards of $100,000, and allocates $1 million annually through a quarterly application process. Successful companies are required to repay the fund either through direct repayment plus a success percentage or through an equity position.

Over the past decade, more than 200 awards valued at nearly $12 million have been made to start-up companies. In turn, these companies have attracted more than $350 million in follow-up investments from private sources, created more than 900 jobs, and supported 250 internships. Through its fund replenishment requirement of companies receiving an award, the Innovation Fund continues to fuel the region's entrepreneurial ecosystem while acquiring significant discretionary dollars as equity positions are liquidated.[28]

ANTICIPATING THE FUTURE

Community colleges are feeling pressure from multiple angles. Resources are stretched to the limit and employees are maxed out on workload and productivity. Students' needs are becoming increasingly complex and competitors increasingly aggressive. National organizations are initiating reform efforts that cost money. Research continues to evolve about the need for change and new business models. And yet, for the most part, our colleges operate on the same model they did thirty years ago. If new models are needed and fundamental change is inevitable, community colleges need to build new capacity within their organization; the most important of which is strategic thinking.

At the 2013 annual meeting of the American Association of Community Colleges, Bill Gates delivered a keynote about the future of higher education. Based on the insights he had gained through his tenure as CEO of Microsoft and more recently with the Bill and Melinda Gates Foundation, he delineated major trends challenging colleges and major changes underway. It was almost overwhelming to hear him speak with confidence and certainty as he tied multiple trends together into a feasible future. I was sitting next to Pat Carter from the Center for Community College Development. She leaned over to me and whispered, "Do you have a group of faculty at your college tracking these trends and thinking about the future?" My blood ran cold because as much attention as we give to the future, I felt the college was not systematically thinking about the future.

In this day and age, every community college should have a futures council or an organized group of some kind that works beyond the three-to-five-year horizon of a typical strategic planning council to systematically scan the external environment on an ongoing basis. As Jim Collins observes, leaders must model a sort of productive paranoia by constantly asking "what if?" and building ongoing scenarios to anticipate the future.[29] MVCC's futuring mechanism is called "Hawkvision" (MVCC's mascot is a Hawk)—a group of faculty and staff that meet biweekly to study the future and promote innovation.

Through Hawkvision's analysis, insights, and recommendations, the college has an increased capacity for future-oriented conversation and action, as the group provides a continuous influx of new ideas that support cultural transformation. With a capacity to anticipate emerging trends and issues, conversations start to change. When Hawkvision assembled a panel of elementary school teachers to gain insights about what was happening in elementary school classrooms, movement toward flipped classrooms, open educational resources, and group work among faculty noticeably increased in a matter of months. The conversation took those trends from news headlines to campus action that intensified development efforts at the college.

Hawkvision activities have served as a stimulus for innovation grants awarded through the MVCC Foundation by prompting white paper development in various areas of the college to capture new ideas and flesh them out in preparation for grant opportunities. Over the past five years, grant activity has significantly increased to more than five times the dollars under management than were being managed seven years earlier. Hawkvision members regularly attend Strategic Horizon Network colloquia to create a natural link between the forward-thinking ideas and experiences of colloquia and prototyping them on campus in the MVCC culture.

Montgomery College, also a Strategic Horizon Network institution, has a similar but different anticipation mechanism called Innovation Works (IW). The purpose of IW is to act as a think-and-do tank that creates "a safe space to extend opportunities for students, staff, faculty, students, and community to develop the taste and capacity for mission-driven innovation and to proactively respond to the challenges facing higher education."[30] IW is a dynamic group of faculty and staff that leverages the professional development infrastructure of the college to offer special events, spotlight current innovations, promote the internal innovation grant process, and engage the entire college community in fostering innovations to advance Montgomery's mission.

Community colleges that thrive in the future will find ways to pay close attention to innovations and platforms that are likely to disrupt existing models of higher education. By actively scanning the environment, leaders and staff will move more quickly to address changing expectations of stakeholders and shifting workplace and societal demands. Forces are already moving at a pace where responding rather than anticipating constitutes failure.

To anticipate change and position themselves for a fast-moving and complex future, community colleges will need to revisit organizational structures and develop hybrid models that are distributed and agile. New and old power will balance in these structures and will fundamentally change cultural dynamics within colleges of the future. Networks will play a significant role in leveraging resources to create new opportunities and in amplifying the impact community colleges make in their communities.

All of these changes will be enhanced for colleges that develop an entrepreneurial mind-set, increase their tolerance for risk, and pursue new and unprecedented ventures that challenge the comfort level of internal stakeholders by creating new dynamics and stretching organizational boundaries. Finally, community colleges must create a culture of anticipation by developing more sophisticated mechanisms to scan and understand trends and shifting external dynamics in order to proactively position themselves for a dynamic future.

The pace of change has greatly accelerated since the turn of the twenty-first century. This intensified pressure amplifies the importance of culture on a daily basis. And just as culture is like a river requiring adept navigation, perhaps most of all, it requires courage to lead in these turbulent times. As Margaret Wheatley cites the words attributed to an elder of the Hopi Nation in Arizona,

> There is a river flowing now very fast. It is so great and swift that there are those who will be afraid. They will try to hold on to the shore. They will feel they are being torn apart and will suffer greatly. Know the river has its destination. The elders say we must let go of the shore, push off into the middle of the river, keep our eyes open, and our heads above the water.
>
> And I say, see who is in there with you and celebrate. At this time in history, we are to take nothing personally, least of all ourselves. For the moment that we do, our spiritual growth and journey come to a halt.
>
> The time of the one wolf is over. Gather yourselves! Banish the word "struggle" from your attitude and your vocabulary. All that we do now must be done in a sacred manner and in celebration.
>
> We are the ones we've been waiting for.[31]

NOTES

1. Joanna Stern, "Jeff Bezos: A Down-to-Earth CEO Reaching for the Stars," ABC News, September 25, 2013. https://abcnews.go.com/Technology/jeff-bezos-amazons-earth-ceo-reaches-stars/story?id=20363682. Website accessed March 20, 2018.

2. MIT OpenCourseWare site. https://ocw.mit.edu/about/our-history/ (accessed June 7, 2017).

3. Shah, D. "MOOCs Started Out Completely Free. Where Are They Now?" April 20, 2017. https://www.edsurge.com/news/2017-04-20-moocs-started-out-completely-free-where-are-they-now (accessed June 18, 2017).

4. Straumsheim, C. (2015). "MOOCs for (a Year's) Credit." *Inside Higher Education.* April, 23, 2015.

5. Huntemann, N. (2017). "Digital Disruption." Strategic Horizon Network Summer Colloquium. Burlington, VT. June 6, 2017.

6. Selingo, J. (2013). "Colleges Can Still Save Themselves." *Chronicle of Higher Education*. December 2, 2013.

7. "Khan Academy: Model for Future of U.S. Education?" (2012). *CBS News: 60 Minutes*. March 11, 2012.

8. Selbert. R. (2017). "Our Extraordinary Future." Strategic Horizon Network Summer Colloquium. Burlington, VT. June 5, 2017.

9. Singer, N. (2017). "How Google Took Over the Classroom." *New York Times*. May 13, 2017.

10. A. Weiss. (2017). Personal communication. June 21, 2017.

11. He, L. (2013). "Google's Secrets of Innovation: Empowering Employees." *Forbes*. March 29, 2013. https://www.forbes.com/sites/laurahe/2013/03/29/googles-secrets-of-innovation-empowering-its-employees/#d31eae457e7b (accessed August 12, 2017).

12. Singer, N. (2017). "How Google Took Over the Classroom."

13. "United States Forgotten Middle." (2017). National Skills Coalition. Washington, DC. February 6, 2017.

14. Flatiron School. www.flatironschool.com/outcomes/ (accessed July 6, 2017).

15. Sydow, D., and Alfred. R. L. (2014). *Re-Visioning Community Colleges*. Lanham, MD: Rowman & Littlefield, 133.

16. Johnson, S. (2010). *Where Good Ideas Come From: The Natural History of Innovation*. New York. Riverhead Books.

17. Satell, G. (2017). "4 Types of Innovation and the Problems They Solve." *Harvard Business Review*. June 21, 2017.

18. Kotter, J. (2014). *Accelerate: Building Strategic Agility for a Faster Moving World*. Boston: Harvard Business Review Press.

19. Sheridan, R. (2013). *Joy, Inc.* New York: Penguin.

20. Alfred, R. A. (2015). "The Future." Strategic Horizon Colloquium. Ann Arbor, MI. June 3, 2015.

21. Ibid.

22. Katz, N., Lazer, D., Arrow, H., and Contractor, N. (2004). "Network Theory and Small Groups." *Small Group Research* 35 (3), June 1, 2004. 307–32.

23. Alfred. (2015). "The Future."

24. "Innovations in the Field: Bronx Opportunity Network." (2016). JobsFirstNYC. New York. November, 2016.

25. C. Haynes. (2017). Personal communication. July 12, 2017.

26. D. Sears. (2017). Personal communication. July 12, 2017.

27. D. Rogers. (2017). Personal Communication. June 26, 2017.

28. T. Green. (2017). Personal communication. August 4, 2017.

29. Collins, J. (2011). *Great by Choice*. New York: HarperCollins.

30. "Innovation Works." Montgomery College. http://cms.montgomerycollege.edu/EDU/Department.aspx?id=74516 (accessed July 8, 2017).

31. Wheatley, M. (2011). "Perseverance: Leadership in Turbulent Times." October 19, 2011. https://www.youtube.com/watch?v=9nRj_ovvUGE&list=PLuWlJWSiXRJMVHGtl0R

uuG9u7OL8YGU2H&index=4.

Appendix A

Cultural Leadership Orientation and 100-Day Action Plan, Mohawk Valley Community College

GUIDING POINTS

- Schedule a conversation with anyone who works at the college and ask them the eight questions listed below. Do not schedule these meetings in YOUR office—go there.
- Keep all your notes on a single notepad so you can refer back to them and more easily develop themes from your conversations.
- Build your list of recurring names of the most respected people and develop solid working relationships with them in the next few months.
- Build your list of people to talk to until you have spoken to about twenty-five individuals and ask them all the same questions so you can identify themes and quickly map the culture.
- Within three weeks, complete all of these meetings and develop an action plan for what you plan to accomplish in the next one hundred calendar days.
- Discuss your action plan with your supervisor and make it happen.

QUESTIONS

1. How would you describe the organizational culture of the college?

2. What are people concerned I might do?
3. What are people concerned I might not do?
4. What are the top three things that should change and why?
5. What are the top three things that should be preserved and why?
6. What advice do you have for me to keep in mind and be successful here?
7. Who are the three most respected people at college and why?

    a. Who are the three people you think it's most important that I talk to in the next thirty days?

Adapted from *You're in Charge—Now What?* by Thomas J. Neff. (2005). New York: Crown Publishing.

CONSIDERATIONS FOR ADMINISTRATIVE APPOINTMENTS

1. If you have been promoted, what are the implications for your need to balance breadth and depth, delegate, influence, communicate, and exhibit leadership presence?
2. If you are new to the organization, how will you orient yourself to the culture, identify and connect with key stakeholders, clarify expectations, and adapt to the new setting? What is the right balance between adapting to the new situation and trying to alter it?
3. What has made you successful so far in your career? Can you succeed in your new position by relying solely on those strengths? If not, what are the critical skills you need to develop?
4. Are there aspects of your new job that are critical to success that you prefer not to focus on? Why? How will you compensate for your potential blind spot?
5. How can you ensure that you make the mental leap into the new position? From whom might you seek advice and counsel on this? What other activities might help you do this?

Manage Up from the Start

1. *Don't stay away.* If you have a boss who doesn't reach out to you, or with whom you have uncomfortable interactions, you will have to reach out yourself. Otherwise, you risk potentially crippling communication gaps. It may feel good to be given a lot of rope, but resist the urge to take it. Get on your boss's calendar regularly. Be sure your boss is aware of the issues you face and that you are aware of the

issues you face and that you are aware of her expectations, especially whether and how they're shifting.

2. *Don't surprise your boss.* It's no fun bringing your boss bad news. However, most bosses consider it a far greater sin not to report emerging problems early enough. Worst of all is for your boss to learn about a problem from someone else. It's usually best to give your new boss at least a heads-up as soon as you become aware of a developing problem.

3. *Don't approach your boss only with problems.* That said, you don't want to be perceived as bringing nothing but problems for your boss to solve. You also need to have plans for how you will proceed. This emphatically does not mean that you must fashion full-blown solutions: The outlay of time and effort to generate solutions can easily lure you down the rocky road to surprising your boss. The key here is to give some thought to how to address the problem—even if it is only gathering more information—and to your role and the help you will need. (This is a good thing to keep in mind in dealing with direct reports, too. It can be dangerous to say, "Don't bring me problems, bring me solutions." Far better is, "Don't just bring me problems, bring me plans for how we can begin to address them.")

4. *Don't run down your checklist.* There is a tendency, even for senior leaders, to use meetings with a boss as an opportunity to run through your checklist of what you've been doing. Sometimes this is appropriate, but it is rarely what your boss needs or wants to hear. You should assume she wants to focus on the most important things you're trying to do and how she can help. Don't go without at most three things you really need to share or on which you need action.

5. *Don't expect your boss to change.* You and your new boss may have very different working styles. You may communicate in different ways, motivate in different ways, and prefer different levels of detail in overseeing your direct reports. But it's your responsibility to adapt to your boss's style; you need to adapt your approach to work with your boss's preferences.

DOs

1. *Clarify expectations early and often.* Begin managing expectations from the moment you consider taking a new role. Focus on expectations during the interview process. You are in trouble if your boss expects you to fix things fast when you know the business has serious structural problems. It's wise to get bad news on the table early and to lower unrealistic expectations. Then check in regularly to make sure your boss's expectations have not shifted. Revisiting expectations is

especially important if you're onboarding from the outside and don't have a deep understanding of the culture and politics.

2. *Take 100 percent responsibility for making the relationship work.* This is the flip side of "don't stay away." Don't expect your boss to reach out or to offer you the time and support you need. It's best to begin by assuming that it's on your shoulders to make the relationship work. If your boss meets you partway, it will be a welcome surprise.

3. *Negotiate timelines for diagnosis and action planning.* Don't let yourself get caught up immediately in firefighting or be pressured to make calls before you're ready. Buy yourself some time, even if it's only a few weeks, to diagnose the new organization and come up with an action plan.

4. *Aim for early wins in areas important to the boss.* Whatever your own priorities, figure out what your boss cares about most. What are his priorities and goals and how do your actions fit into this picture? Once you know, aim for early results in those areas. One good way is to focus on three things that are important to your boss and discuss what you're doing about them every time you interact. In that way, your boss will feel ownership of your success.

5. *Pursue good marks from those whose opinions your boss respects.* Your new boss's opinion of you will be based in part on direct interactions and in part on what she hears about you from trusted others. Your boss will have preexisting relationships with people who are now your peers and possibly your subordinates. You needn't curry favor with the people your boss trusts. Simply be alert to the multiple channels through which information and opinion about you will reach your boss.

6. *Establish momentum.* Identify three or four early wins on issues where you can act fairly quickly with modest expenditures to yield visible operational and financial gains.

Plan for Five Conversations

Your relationship with your new boss will be built through an ongoing dialogue. Several subjects belong at the center of this dialogue. It's valuable to include plans for five specific conversations about transition-related subjects in your one-hundred-day plan.

1. *The situational diagnosis conversation*: Seek to understand how your boss assesses the situation you have inherited.

2. *The expectations conversation*: Understand and negotiate expectations. What does your boss need you to do in the short term and in the medium term? What will constitute success? How will your perfor-

mance be measured? When? Remember to underpromise and overdeliver.

3. *The resource conversation*: What do you need to be successful? What do you need your boss to do?

4. *The style conversation*: What forms of communication does your boss prefer, and for what? Face-to-face? Voice? Electronic? How often? What kinds of decisions does he want to be consulted on and what kinds of calls can you make on your own?

5. *The personal development conversation*: Toward the end of your one hundred days, you can begin to discuss how you're doing and what your developmental priorities should be.

Adapted from *The First 90 Days* by Michael D. Watkins (Boston: Harvard Business School Publishing, 2013).

Appendix B

Strategies, Programs, and Events to Build Connections, Community, and a More Cohesive Culture

PRESIDENT AND SENIOR LEADER EXPOSURE

1. President meeting individually with all new full-time employees within first five months
2. Dessert receptions or coffee hours with President's Cabinet and all full-time employees with birthdays each month or some other organizing principle to create random social interactions
3. Student lunches or receptions with the president and/or vice presidents
4. Town hall meetings with students in the residence halls (if available) each semester
5. President and vice presidents attending monthly college senate/assembly meetings or meetings with each governance body leader or executive committee
6. Senior team members attending regularly student assembly/congress meetings
7. Personalized years of service recognition in lieu of one big end-of-year recognition
8. Monthly labor roundtables to keep communication open with union leadership
9. Annual joint cabinet/senate (or major governance entity) retreats
10. Handwritten notes and/or birthday cards from the president
11. President and senior team members attending student-oriented events
12. President and senior team members hosting events at their homes for faculty and staff

SOCIALLY ENGINEERED INTERDEPARTMENTAL CONNECTIONS

1. Professional development days for faculty and staff
2. New Faculty Institute cohort program with monthly workshops
3. Leadership Academy cohort program with monthly workshops
4. Two-day summer retreats for all administrators
5. Day-of-service opportunities or community volunteer group
6. Monthly campus conversations, brown-bag lunches or town halls with faculty and staff
7. Workplace by Facebook social-media platform for internal communications
8. Affinity groups sponsored by a diversity council or similar governance entity
9. Affinity groups sponsored by a Strengths Council or group advocating Strengths
10. Walking/exercise groups sponsored by an employee wellness council or similar group
11. Faculty and staff and/or student competitions (kickball, volleyball, softball, board games, ugly holiday sweater, etc.)
12. Potluck gatherings in various forms throughout the year
13. Coffee with colleagues (arranged interdepartmental invites)
14. Supporting organic ideas like off-campus happy hours at different local establishments

LARGE GROUP CONVENINGS

1. Fall opening (new academic year kickoff) and spring start all-college gatherings
2. Annual all-college picnics
3. All-college data summits to explore student success data
4. Biannual end of semester celebrations or all-employee gatherings
5. Monthly administrator meetings (randomized seating) with program updates and prompted strategic discussion items

Appendix C

Start Right—Success Program for New Employees, Mohawk Valley Community College

The Start Right Program is comprised of a supervisory-led orientation program and special sessions at the August and January Institutes. The intent is to ensure that all new employees feel welcomed; understand what is expected from them; and feel supported, comfortable and excited about their new position at Mohawk Valley Community College.

START RIGHT PROGRAM PHILOSOPHY

While nearly every position requires special elements with regard to their orientation, a number of information items and actions are essential for all new employees to get started in the most positive and productive manner possible. The following principles guide the design and implementation of this program by making each new employee feel like they are

- welcomed to the college,
- part of a team and belong to a thriving learning community,
- provided with an emotionally intelligent supervisor that supports and cares about them and their success,
- provided with the tools and resources to fulfill their core job responsibilities,
- comfortable and confident in their position from their very first day on the job, and
- off to a productive and meaningful start to their career at MVCC.

Philosophy in Action

For the Start Right Program to significantly shape the organizational culture, each supervisor must understand and fully adhere to the philosophy, guiding principles, and outline to ensure that each component is completed appropriately and in a timely manner.

7–14 Days Prior to First Day—Supervisor Preparations for Arrival (if at all possible)

- Reserve time on your calendar to reflect and prepare for your new employee so you can feel confident in guiding the first day.
- Develop itinerary for first week of activity. Strongly consider breaking things up into 30–60-minute periods throughout the first day and the first week and utilize other staff to lead different segments (i.e., someone else to do the tour, etc.)—making it easier to comprehend and meet colleagues.
- Secure items for "welcome kit."
- Secure access* for all necessary hardware and software (if needed)—open accounts for network, e-mail, SIRS, BANNER, and so forth. (*Access may only be processed after required paperwork is completed and entered by Human Resources.)
- Request key(s) for office and/or position.
- Schedule a time to meet with Human Resources to complete required paperwork. This appointment may be scheduled prior to the first day or on the first day.
- Print out the job description.
- Print out MVCC's mission, vision and core values statements.
- Set up workspace, materials, and/or equipment as appropriate to job responsibilities.
- Identify a primary resource person/mentor in a similar role at the college and talk to this person about serving in that role for the new employee, and advise this resource person/mentor that your new hire will be contacting them. Make arrangements with the resource person/mentor's supervisor as appropriate.
- Draft a notice introduction to the college or work with marketing and communications to do so.
- Order a name tag as well as business cards and/or nameplate, if appropriate.
- Consider creating a small reference sheet of important phone numbers and contacts that are key for the particular position.
- Reserve time on your calendar during the second week to continue orientation.
- Reserve additional time to check in and review various topics on a weekly basis for the first two months on the job.

Day 1 (all positions)

Remember that this is more about engagement and support than just running through content on a checklist. You are setting the tone from this point forward.

- Keep it light by allowing the new employee time in the office to get acclimated.
- Make introductions—within the department and key office personnel.
- Provide the standard "welcome kit" and add any pieces you'd like.
- Review itinerary you have planned for their first week.
- Review MVCC's mission, vision, and core values statements and discuss how their position contributes to carry out the college's mission, vision, and core values.
- Remind the new employee to obtain parking decal and photo identification (HR provides information with required paperwork).
- Show where bathrooms are, explain food-service options, show bookstore and various office locations on campus.
- Review your expectations and solicit their expectations.
- Review the professional expectations:

  - Work hours, breaks, lunches, timesheets reporting absences and re- questing time off, overtime requests and overload, ajar period
  - Parking
  - Work attire
  - Communication expectations—phone and e-mail etiquette, personal telephone calls, social media, professionalism
  - Review confidentiality and Family Educational Rights and Privacy Act (FERPA).
  - Stress the importance of civility in the workplace.
  - Work area organization and maintenance
  - Other professional expectations of importance

- Review these tools and resources:

  - Keys
  - Telephone and voicemail
  - Copier
  - Computer, printer
  - Supplies
  - Software such as BANNER, Argos, Microsoft Products, OnBase, De- greeWorks, SIRS, and so forth.
  - Provide instructions on how to gain access to software/systems and utilize.

- Provide introductions to key team members in external offices or office members with whom the person will work with most.
- Provide access to the Employee Directory.
- Other professional expectations of importance.

- Review safety measures and/or procedures:

  - Storage of personal items
  - Departmental safety
  - Public safety resources
  - Health office resources reporting workplace injuries
  - Evacuation plans
  - Fire extinguishers
  - Automated External Defibrillator (AED)
  - Areas of refuge
  - NY Alert in SIRS
  - Behavioral Evaluation Response Team (BERT)
  - Other safety measures and/or procedures

Day 1 (optional depending on position)

- Provide a training schedule for at least one week with different colleagues, as appropriate.
- Review cultural leadership orientation and questions and identify first three (3) people.
- For union positions, provide the appropriate collective bargaining agreement (CBA).
- Arrange and communicate training time(s) for any technology-based tools essential to the new employee's job.
- Procedure and process for internal and external off-site work location(s) (internal: Educational Opportunity Center—EOC, external: Defense Finance and Accounting Services—DFAS, etc.).
- For faculty:

  - Provide texts, course outlines, sample syllabi, standard PowerPoint files, campus and classrooms maps, and so forth.
  - Review Blackboard resources, and so forth.
  - Tour academic labs, if appropriate.
  - Review New Faculty Institute (all four years) programming. Make sure teaching schedules and calendars are synchronized to maximize their attendance.

Days 2–5 (all positions)

- Review the mission, goals, and performance metrics (if appropriate) for the center, department, or office and outline how the new employee's role complements those of other team members or fulfills an important aspect of the area's mission.
- Introduce the new employee to someone who performs the same or similar role, a "go-to" colleague who serves as a resource person/mentor.
- Provide a list of commonly used MVCC terms and acronyms—Argos, CWCC, ATD, and so forth—that they may encounter in their position.
- As part of a larger conversation about employee enrichment and recognition, provide information about any upcoming institutes or trainings that they should or might consider attending. Review where training information is available.
- Provide a campus tour and meetings with offices they will work with collaboratively.
- Review the college's two campuses—Rome, Utica, and other sites as applicable.
- Schedule a time for the employee to get their picture taken in the marketing and communications studio.
- Review the structure of the organization and their primary team.

Days 2–5 (optional, depending on position)

- Review finance procedures—for example, signatures and authorizations, budget codes, and processes, and travel and mileage, if appropriate.
- Explain and review required paperwork—travel requests and so forth.
- Review MVCC's website.
- Explain the governance system at MVCC by reviewing the College Senate, councils, and workgroup websites with the new employee.
- Provide an overview and/or information on the Center for Corporate and Community Education (CCED), along with contact information for additional questions.
- Provide an overview and/or information on the MVCC Foundation, along with contact information for additional questions.

Months 1–6

- New employee meets regularly (as appropriate) with supervisor to review Start Right information (to minimize overload) and assess progress, barriers, and comfort level with responsibilities, and provide feedback.
- New employee meets with the president for twenty-minute personal conversation.

- Supervisor encourages attendance at August or January Institute workshops (during first year):

    - MVCC—past, present, and future/values lunch with President's Cabinet
    - MVCC—strengths for new employees
    - MVCC—the emotionally intelligent workplace

Initiated Fall 2014

Index

About the Author

Randall VanWagoner, PhD, serves as the fifth president of Mohawk Valley Community College—a position he has held since July 1, 2007. He currently is serving his second term as chair of the New York Community Colleges Association of Presidents, a position he has held since 2015.

He holds a PhD and MA from the Higher Education program at the University of Michigan–Ann Arbor; a BA in communications from Oakland University in Rochester, Michigan; and before transferring to Oakland, was a two-sport athlete at Mott Community College in Flint, Michigan.

Dr. VanWagoner previously held positions of chief academic officer, chief student affairs officer, registrar, director of Institutional Research and Planning, and research analyst at community colleges in Nebraska, Colorado, and Michigan. He is an active evaluation-team chair for the Middle States Commission on Higher Education and an executive coach for senior community college administrators. Dr. VanWagoner has been instrumental in the development of the national Strategic Horizons Network of community colleges—serving as the co-facilitator of the seven-college Network focused on learning about disruptive innovation and vibrant organizational cultures outside of higher education.

He currently serves on the national Jobs for the Future Policy Trust and is a former president of the National Council for Instructional Administrators. Dr. VanWagoner also serves as the co-chair of the Vision 2020 initiative for Oneida County and as a member of the board of directors for the Boilermaker Road Race, Community Foundation of Herkimer and Oneida Counties, Mohawk Valley Economic Growth and Development Enterprises, and the Northeast UAS Airspace Integration Research Alliance.

Dr. VanWagoner is married to Jennifer VanWagoner. They have two daughters, Lauren and Emily.